From Boston to Berlin

From Boston to Berlin

A Journey through World
War II in Images and Words

CHRISTOPHER E. MAURIELLO
AND ROLAND J. REGAN, JR.

Purdue University Press
West Lafayette, Indiana

05 04 03 02 01   5 4 3 2 1

⊖ The paper used in this book meets the minimum requirements of American National Standard for Information Sciences—Permanence of Paper for Printed Library Materials, ANSI Z39.48-1992.

Printed in the United States of America

Library of Congress Cataloging-in-Publication Data applied for

Contents

Preface

IN THE SUMMER OF 1994, while at his mother's apartment, Roland came upon a box of photos that his father had taken during his service in World War II between 1943 and 1945. While he had known of the existence of these photographs for over thirty years, the exact location of them was not known until then. While inventorying these photos, medals, and other memorabilia for the first time in nearly twenty years, Roland began to remember the few but poignant remarks that his father had made about his World War II experience. His father would recollect the V1 "Buzz Bombs" flying overhead on cold late November and December days and nights in Belgium in 1944; Luftwaffe ME 262s (jet fighters) strafing Company A near the Roer River; and German snipers shooting at Company A members who were building a bridge across the Sieg River in March 1945. As these memories of his father's wartime experience ebbed and flowed in his mind, Roland's appreciation of the meaning and impact these photographs had on his father's memory of the war, as well as his understanding of his father's role in the twentieth century's most important event, began to crystallize. As Roland looked through these black-and-white memories of World War II, he began to feel a commitment to his deceased father and his generation to make these photos public so that others could share this wartime experience.

Between the summers of 1995 and 1998, Roland began to construct how he wanted his father's photos to be viewed and preserved for later generations. In 1997, he contacted several commercial and university publishers to learn more about what steps he would need to take in order to publish his father's photos in a commercial illustrative form. Simultaneously, he contacted several national universities and colleges to possibly donate these photographs to their history departments for use in research and teaching World War II. To his surprise, the response from both publishers and universities was very encouraging. However, organizing and presenting such a collection of photos proved to be a labor of love, as his weekends and evenings during this period were consumed selecting, scanning, and editing hundreds of original photos.

During that time Roland was teaching several business courses at Salem State College in Salem, Massachusetts. In the summer of 1998, he contacted the history department to notify them of his interest in donating a digitized CD-ROM version of his father's photos for use by the history department. His message was forwarded to Christopher Mauriello, the modern European historian for the department.

In a strikingly parallel way, Chris had been searching for ways to make his father's private war documents accessible to the public. In 1993, while a Ph.D. candidate in history at Brown University, he was cleaning out the basement of his aunt's home in Massachusetts when he discovered a box of World War II letters that his father had written to his family back in Boston between 1943 and 1945. As a side project to his research on modern European history, he began to read, transcribe, annotate, and historically contextualize the over 250 letters he discovered. He discussed the project with colleagues in the historical field and editors of major university presses.

With these shared commitments, we met for coffee to introduce ourselves and review each other's collections. Immediately we recognized the powerful parallels between the images and the words. We soon discovered that the parallels ran even deeper. Both of our fathers were sons of European immigrants that settled and lived in the Boston area. Roland J. Regan, Sr., was of Irish descent and was raised in Lynn, Massachusetts. Frederick J. Mauriello was of Italian descent and was raised in Dorchester and Revere, Massachusetts. Both volunteered for active service in the U.S. Army in 1943. Between the summer of 1944 and 1945 both experienced similar paths in combat against the German army—Roland in the First Army, 348th Army Engineering Combat Battalion, Company A; and Frederick in the 309th Field Artillery Battalion 78th Division. The parallels between these two wartime experiences form the basis of this book.

In May 2000, the Boston College history department and the Bapst Library on campus accepted and became the official custodian of some one hundred and fifty of Roland's father's original photographs for use by historians and researchers at the university.

While we have added a brief narrative history and captions to the photographs and the letters to provide the necessary historical context, we hope that the original documents speak for themselves. We hope they do justice to the memory of the wartime experiences of our fathers and their "greatest generation." Furthermore, to commemorate our respective fathers' memories, we intend to develop two scholarship funds in their names, from the revenues generated from the sales of this book, to assist deserving students from Lynn and Revere who attend Boston College. We feel our commitment to these two scholarships for future generations is in keeping with our fathers' mutual commitments to their generation. More information concerning these scholarship funds will be forthcoming via our website at: www.bostontoberlin.org.

—Roland J. Regan, Jr.
—Christopher E. Mauriello

Acknowledgments

AUTHORS INCUR A GREAT MANY DEBTS writing books. This was particularly true in our case.

Roland J. Regan, Jr., would like to acknowledge his deepest gratitude and sincerest appreciation to the late Roland James Regan, Sr., for his uncanny foresight, sensitivity, and understanding of the historical significance in the events that were unfolding before and around him between 1943 and 1945. His unique vantage point and perspective of World War II are evident in all of his photographs during this period. These photos are a living testament to the common soldiers whose daily lives are reflected against this tumultuous backdrop. Lastly, Roland Jr. thanks him as a father, husband, and friend whose strength of character and positive image are a beacon of light that shines as brightly today for those of his issue, matrimony, and acquaintance. The late Patrick J. and Margaret (Lombard) Regan, Roland Sr.'s parents, amply prepared their son to undertake and successfully meet the rigors he would face during his wartime experience and inspired him to photograph these experiences for generations to come. Mary Teresa (Hunt) Regan, Roland Jr.'s mother, demonstrated tireless encouragement, understanding, indomitable spirit, and a positive attitude, which made the six-year development of this book, as well as other projects, feasible over the years. Roland Jr. is grateful to his sisters, Paulette Teresa (Regan) Puleo and Sheila Ann (Regan) Ohanesian, for their collective encouragement and understanding during the development of this book; to his nephews and nieces, Todd Regan Ohanesian, Scott Regan Ohanesian, Reaghan Lee Puleo, and Ashley Kate Puleo, for their collective encouragement; to his uncle, Robert L. Regan, for his contributions and encouragement; to Patricia (Regan) Benson and James Regan, Roland Sr.'s niece and nephew, for their collective contribution to this book.

Further thanks are due to James W. Dunn, Ph.D., historian for the U.S. Army Corps of Engineers, for his timely research and assistance with sources; to Robert K. O'Neill, Ph.D., archivist for the Burns Library, Boston College; and Professor John Heineman, Ph.D., History Department, Boston College, for their professional services and support in archiving the Roland Regan, Sr., Collection of World War II Photographs and Military Regalia at the John J. Burns Library of Rare Books and Special Collections at Boston College; to Robert Stroud of The Regan Group in New York City, for his counsel and encouragement in finding publishers for Roland Sr.'s photos and story; to Paul

Ferguson and Paul Amato of RePro Video, Inc., for their professional assistance and expert technical knowledge in completing the Quick-Time CD-ROM movie of these photographs with an accompanying musical score for this publication; and to Don LeGere, formerly of the Salem State College media department, for his expert technical assistance, creativity, and patience in digitizing and editing the original photographs and for the creation of the initial movie video containing these photographs.

~

CHRISTOPHER MAURIELLO IS DEEPLY indebted to the people whose lives, work, and encouragement made this book possible, especially his father, Frederick J. Mauriello, Sr., whose "words" in the form of war letters inspired the author to share his family history with a broader reading public. Frederick's sensitive reflections on family, friends, war, civilians, politics, and society and his constant good humor represent the man as he lived—and continues to live—as son, brother, soldier, husband, father, and grandfather. Christopher is grateful to his mother, Jacqueline Mauriello, for her love, encouragement, and support and for forwarding important letters, documents, and photos that made this book possible; to his grandparents Angelina and Eugene Mauriello, for risking their son in a world war and for inspiring him to write with such love and respect back home; to his aunts, Edna Mauriello, Marie Smolinsky, and Dorothy Foley, for their ongoing correspondence with their brother Frederick throughout his service, which formed the "other half" of the letters, and also for their love, support, and encouragement with this book; and to his brothers and sisters, Mary Angela, Frederick, Margaret, and Lisa, for their encouragement and support of all my work over the years.

Further thanks are due to Donna Davis, who indexed, transcribed, edited, and digitized every letter in the collection during the summer of 1999 and whose organization, ideas, and encouragement were invaluable; to Stanley Polny, historian for the 78th Division, and Bill Parsons, editor for *The Flash* publication of the 78th Division, for their assistance early in the process by providing invaluable historical resources on the 309th Field Artillery Battalion and their constant support of the project.

Finally, Christopher would like to thank his wife, Ann, and his three children, Alyssa, Michael, and Matthew, for their love, good cheer, time, and patience while this book was being written.

~

IN CLOSING, THE AUTHORS WOULD LIKE to add a special thanks to Margaret Hunt and Thomas Bacher from Purdue University Press, for their vision, faith, and professional expertise in the development and production of this book. They would also like to thank Michael Saporito of GMSG Web Design, who creatively designed, developed, and continues to maintain the *From Boston to Berlin* Web site.

Most of all, the authors would like to acknowledge the men and women who served in World War II and their families on the home front. It is to them, the generation that gave so much in the defense of freedom and democracy, that this book is dedicated.

From Boston to Berlin

Introduction

Parallel Lives

Ordinary Men in Extraordinary Circumstances

This book is about strangers. Two men, Roland J. Regan, Sr., and Frederick J. Mauriello, Sr., who never met each other, talked to each other, or were even aware of each other's existence. Yet, like millions of Americans of their generation, their lives converged around one of this century's greatest events, World War II. The war transformed the world. Democracy triumphed over the evils of fascism, but not before the fascists had demonstrated the depth of man's inhumanity to man. Geopolitics was recast into the Cold War, where former allies became deadly superpower enemies. America emerged out of the prewar Great Depression to postwar prosperity and consumerism. But the power of the war to transform was most evident in its effects on the men and women who fought in it. To paraphrase an oft-quoted line, it took ordinary men and put them in extraordinary circumstances. It turned ordinary young men like Roland Regan and Frederick Mauriello into what Stephen Ambrose aptly labeled "citizen soldiers."[1] In doing so it forged a common generational experience and made parallel lives out of separate lives.

This book is an attempt to tell the story of parallel lives through the unique historical record that these two World War II veterans left behind. Roland Regan photographed his experience of war. The photographs that he took as a soldier in the 348th Engineer Combat Battalion, Company A, provide never-before published images of World War II. They visually document his journey from the Allied preparations for the D-Day invasion in Swansea, Wales, to Omaha Beach, to the laying of bridges across Germany's rivers for the Allied advance into Germany, to the collapse of the Third Reich and the gruesome discoveries of the Wöbbelin concentration camp near Ludwigslust. They are not professional photographs, but rather the snapshots taken by a soldier amidst the constant action, chaos, and destruction of war. But this is what makes them compelling historical and documentary evidence.

Roland's (left) and Frederick's formal portraits, taken in 1943, reveal the confidence and optimism with which they faced their wartime duties.

They depict the war through the eyes of an ordinary soldier. Moreover, most of the photographs were not developed until after Roland returned to the United States at the end of the war and never passed through military censors. They are the unedited glimpses into the raw experiences of a soldier's life as he encounters war for the first time.

The lens captures what Roland finds interesting, significant, and meaningful, not what official military publicists, officers, or civilian photojournalists might find expedient for the war effort. Therefore, the photographs include a variety of World War II scenes: sweeping shots of the post-D-Day invasion documenting the massive destruction caused by this event; an engineering division building roads and constructing bridges in combat situations; German soldiers surrendering to advancing U.S. troops; devastated German armaments, cities, and civilians; the horrors of the Holocaust. They also document the lives and experiences of ordinary soldiers between battles: group shots of soldiers forged into friendship through war; Roland and his fellow combat engineers on leave in Paris after its liberation; and a rare photograph of Roland posing with champion boxer Rocky Marciano.

Frederick Mauriello wrote about his experience of war. His letters were accompanied by a few photographs that he sent back to his family in the Boston area while serving as a radio operator in the 78th Division's 309th Field Artillery Battalion. They provide unique insight into the observations, thoughts, and emotions of an ordinary soldier. The letters document his journey from basic training in the United States to the muddy fields of Belgium; from the horrific combat of the Battle of the Bulge to the crossing of the Remagen Bridge; and finally to the collapse and occupation of Germany. Like Regan's photographs, this unique collection of over two hundred and forty letters documents the war in powerful ways. They are not the letters of an intellectual, novelist, or journalist consciously prepared for posterity or historical mem-

oirs. Instead, they are heartfelt and thoughtful personal letters of a homesick young man writing to his mother, father, and three sisters in Revere, Massachusetts, about his powerful experiences of war in a strange, far-off land. The subject matter of the letters, however, is not merely personal. They provide an unusually articulate representation of the thoughts, ideas, and experiences of an ordinary working-class young man during World War II. They reveal the anxiety, fear, and exhilaration before and during battle; the comradeship forged at the front between brothers in arms; the recognition of the human and physical costs of war; the relationship between GIs and German civilians; and finally, the meaning of World War II to those who fought in it as well as to the broader history of humanity. Like the photographs, the letters document a moving yet realistic version of the war and the role of ordinary men in combat.

This book, therefore, is a social history of World War II. Its goal is to capture the essence of war as social experience. While it documents battles, movements of troops, and the strategies of war, it does so through the eyes of the ordinary citizen soldiers who actually lived these military events. What were the emotions and opinions of the men before, during, and after battles? What actually happened "on the ground" during the war? What new perspective does this view shed on World War II and the men who fought it? Fundamentally, the book attempts to provide a perspective on history from the "bottom up"— seeking to understand and interpret history from the lives and thoughts of common people, who are often silent or forgotten in official histories.

The book is also a documentary history of America's involvement in World War II. The photographs and letters document the lives of two men as they experience their generation's most significant event. As historical documents the photographs and letters provide never-before published evidence of the day-to-day life and experiences of com-

family in the postwar prosperity of the new America. However, it was the Depression and World War II that defined their lives and the lives of their entire generation. Their photographs and the letters tell that story and how the war shaped their generation's outlook on life. They display the combination of patriotism, love of family and friends, respect for tradition, religion, and hard work, the economic anxiety, and cautious hope for the future that defined the "war generation."

Finally, the book is a memoir. The co-authors, Roland Regan, Jr., and Christopher Mauriello, are sons who want to memorialize their fathers' experiences in World War II. Like many children of the war generation, they grew up listening to their parents' stories about the war but only came to recognize the importance of these stories as they matured and experienced their own lives. So this is also a story of parents and children—a meeting of generations. One generation fought hard and paid dear to preserve a way of life and a world that a younger generation would only later come to appreciate.

Ordinary Lives: Biographical Background

Roland James Regan was born in Lynn, Massachusetts, on December 8, 1922. He was the son of two Irish immigrants, Margaret (Lombard) and Patrick J. Regan from Mallow and Skibbereen respectively in County Cork, Ireland. He was the second of four children (Vincent a.k.a.

mon soldiers during wartime. They are unfiltered first-hand evidence that gives new insight into World War II and the men and women who fought in this historical event. Hopefully students, teachers, scholars, and the general public will use these rare documents to reexamine the U.S. soldier's experience of World War II and the social experience of ordinary American citizens.

In important ways the book also contributes to the history of generations of Americans. Roland Regan and Frederick Mauriello lived lives representative of an entire generation. Born in 1922 and 1921 respectively, each was the son of an immigrant family that came to America for a better life. Each came of age during the Great Depression. Each joined the army in 1942, fought in World War II, and lived to raise his

Like many families, the Regans sent more than one son off to war. Left: On leave in April 1943, Roland (center) sits on the back stairs of their home in Lynn with his brothers Pat (on leave from the Navy, which he had joined in June 1942) and Bob (who would join the Navy in late 1945). Right: Roland's brothers Pat and Bob with their future brother-in-law, Chet Whitten (left), in September 1943. Chet and Roland would later run into each other in France (see chapter 2).

Pat, Roland, Peg, and Robert). Patrick was a bus driver for the Eastern Massachusetts Street Railway Company while Margaret worked at home raising her children.

"Rollie," as he was known among his family and friends, was raised during the Roaring Twenties and the Great Depression. Even though the Regans were a working-class family, they were able to avoid most of the severe economic and psychological hardships of the Great Depression, as Patrick maintained his job during this tumultuous economic period. Both his strong Irish immigrant roots and those trying economic times were to shape Roland's view of the world forever. In late 1939, Roland's father, Patrick, became ill with tuberculosis and was hospitalized off and on until his death in January 1942. During this period, Roland and his brother Pat left Lynn English High School to help support his mother and younger siblings. Initially he worked as many

as four different jobs during the course of a week to help his family make ends meet. Some of those jobs between 1940 and 1942 included working as a railroad fireman and a welder at the Quincy Naval Shipyards.

In January 1943 Roland joined the United States Army. In June 1943 he was assigned to the 1st Army, 348th Engineer Combat Battalion, Company A. During this time his battalion trained and prepared for the inevitable invasion of continental Europe by building pontoon bridges and other structures across lakes and rivers at various military camps on the East Coast. Roland received specialized training in welding and metallurgy while stationed at Camp Pickett, Virginia. It was here that he also learned the art and science of bridge building, mine detection, and weapons use for the crucial tasks that awaited him in Europe. In mid-April the 348th was moved to Camp Myles Standish near Taunton, Massachusetts. They continued honing their craft of bridge building by building bridges across several local rivers. On October 30, 1943, the 348th boarded trains from Camp Myles Standish and headed toward Halifax, Canada. On November 2 the battalion set sail on the refitted luxury liner the HMS *Mauretania* to England. On Monday, November 8, the battalion arrived in Liverpool, England, among the first American troops to arrive in this part of Great Britain. In early

December the 348th moved to the seaport town of Swansea, Wales, and continued preparing for the invasion of continental Europe.

It was during this time that Roland further fine-tuned his interest in taking and developing photographs, an interest that allowed him to capture some unique and personal perspectives on World War II. Many of his collection of some two hundred photos spanning April of 1943 through July of 1945 are on display in this book. Immediately after the war Roland contributed photographs used in the pictorial history of the 348th published by the U.S. Army, for which he was duly recognized.

Roland was honorably discharged from the Army, returning to Lynn on October 15, 1945. During his army stint he had sent home three of every four checks to help his mother. When he returned to his prewar job as a welder at the Quincy Naval Shipyard, he continued to support his mother until her death in the autumn of 1950.

Roland attended a reunion of the 150th Engineer Combat Battalion (which combined with the 348th during most of the war) in Boston on May 6, 1947. In July of 1947 he was appointed as a firefighter on the Lynn fire department, where he would spend the next thirty-four years of his life. In June of 1948 Roland took his mother back to Ireland to visit their numerous relatives in Cork. During this period he met Mary Teresa Hunt from Roscommon, Ireland. On April 14, 1951, they were married and had three children: Roland, Jr., Paulette, and Sheila; and four grandchildren, Todd, Reaghan, Scott, and Ashley. Roland returned to Ireland with his young family in June 1965 and visited Ireland with his family numerous times during the next twenty years. He retired from the Lynn fire department as a lieutenant in July 1981. Roland attended his second, and last, 348th reunion in central Connecticut in September 1988. He passed away after a lengthy illness on November 15, 1989.

Frederick Joseph Mauriello, Sr., was born in Boston, Massachusetts, on October 20, 1921. He was the first child and only son of Eugene and Angelina Mauriello, both immigrants from Avellino, Italy. They entered the United States with millions of other southern European immigrants during the first decades of the twentieth century. "Freddy," as he was called in family circles, was followed by three sisters: Edna, born February 27, 1923; Marie, born November 2, 1924; and Dorothy, born February 26, 1927. The Mauriello family initially settled in Dorchester, Massachusetts, a working-class section of Boston. In 1937 they moved to the Beachmont section of Revere, an immediate suburb of Boston. Like many first-generation immigrants, the children assimilated into American culture in the public spaces of

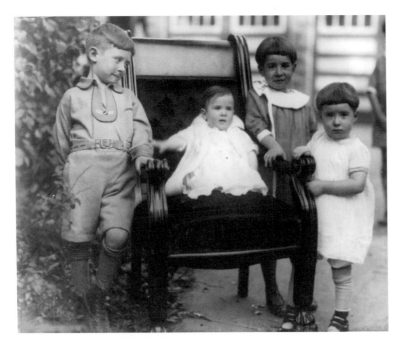

Older brother Frederick Mauriello gazes protectively at his sisters, Dorothy, Edna, and Marie. These extraordinarily close family ties are also evident in the letters he wrote home during the war.

school, work, and civic life. However, they continued to embrace and retain their Italian heritage and their Roman Catholic faith in the home, around the dinner table, and among their close circle of relatives and family friends.

Like many World War II veterans, Frederick and his family were profoundly shaped by the experiences of the Great Depression when the parents and children worked various jobs, pooling their resources to support their family. Like many others, the "Depression experience" reinforced and deepened Frederick's commitment to the importance of family, faith, and friendship. It also created a lifelong focus on economic circumstance, educational achievement, and social position.

Frederick graduated from Revere High School in 1939. As a result of his childhood fascination with radio, he attended Massachusetts Radio School, receiving his radio operator's license. He then worked in the Charlestown Navy Yard installing radio towers and radio systems on a variety of naval vessels. In 1942, following the United States' entry in World War II, Frederick joined the United States Army and was sent to Army Specialized Training Program (ASTP) in electrical engineering at the University of Connecticut and the University of Alabama.

With the Army's need for men with specialized training, Frederick was sent to join the 309th Field Artillery Battalion, Headquarters Battery, as a radio operator directing artillery fire. He trained in Camp Forest, Tennessee, Fort Bragg, North Carolina, and Camp Pickett, Virginia. Frederick and the battalion were sent to Bristol, England, in October 1944 and landed in Le Havre, France, on November 22, 1944. He wrote letters back home to his parents and sisters throughout his military experience, and the letters from 1943 to the end of 1945 are presented in this book.

Frederick was honorably discharged from the Army in early 1946. Like many veterans, he received GI Bill benefits, and graduated with a bachelor's degree from Boston College in 1951 and an M.B.A. from Northeastern University in 1954. He married Jacqueline Santos, a nurse, in 1955. During that same year he began a career with IBM in New York that would last more than thirty years. Frederick and Jacqueline raised five children: Mary Angela, Frederick, Christopher, Margaret, and Lisa in Millbrook, New York. He and his wife live in New York and enjoy nine grandchildren.

Extraordinary Circumstances: Wartime Experiences and History

While these two American lives are remarkably parallel, it is the experience of World War II that formed a common bond. Roland Regan and Frederick Mauriello both fought in World War II in the European Theater of Operations during 1944 and 1945. Roland served with the 348th Engineer Combat Battalion, Company A, which was originally attached to the First Army under the command of General Omar Bradley. Frederick served with the 309th Field Artillery Battalion, Headquarters Battery of the 78th Lightning Division, also attached to the First Army. While they served in very different capacities, Roland as a combat engineer and Frederick as a radio operator, their paths through wartime Europe were parallel in both geographical direction and time. So were their experiences, which are documented so vividly in their photographs and letters. Like millions of other GIs in Europe, both saw combat against Hitler's armies in the major battles of the European Theater. While Roland arrived and fought in Europe three months before Frederick (participating at the D-Day landing in Normandy in June 1944 and fighting toward the breakthrough against the German armies in August of that year), after November 1944 their paths become remarkably similar. Roland and Frederick both participated in the Battle in the Bulge during the winter of 1944–45, fought

Frederick on leave in Revere, Massachusetts, 1943.

as part of an army or a nation at war. This does not mean that ordinary soldiers like Roland and Frederick were oblivious to the larger strategies and goals of World War II or to the historical significance of their military service. Roland's photographs and Frederick's letters demonstrate a keen understanding that each was part of one of history's greatest events and each needed to somehow document it for posterity. Their photographs and letters tell the story of World War II at the immediate battalion level—a war fought by American boys from Boston to California, thrown together by circumstance, united by a combination of fear, bravery, boredom, playfulness, sadness, and triumph.

The brief summary of the combat history of the 348th Engineer Combat Battalion, Company A, and the 309th Field Artillery Battalion, Headquarters Battery, that follows was written with respect to the local experience of war. The history of Roland Regan's experience was reconstructed from Keith Bryan's *Pack Up and Move: A Pictorial History of the 348th Engineer Combat Battalion* as well as the the personal notes of Roland J. Regan, Jr.[2] The history of Frederick Mauriello's experience was taken from *The 309th Field Artillery Battalion: World War II European Theatre of Operations*, published in 1947, and the personal notes of Christopher Mauriello.[3] The summary that follows is by no means an exhaustive history of each of the battalion's wartime service. Instead, it aims to provide a timeline, context, and geographic reference for Roland's photographs and Frederick's letters that make up the main content of the book.

with their battalions across Germany's rivers in the spring of 1945, battled retreating German armies city to city during late April and May, and occupied German territory after the surrender of German forces and the collapse of Nazi Germany in May of 1945.

Not surprisingly, the military experiences of Roland and Frederick represent the general movement of U.S. troops in Europe. However, each of their battalions played a specific role within the larger strategy of Allied operations, and these histories also need to be told. As any veteran can tell you, most soldiers experience war, even a global war such as World War II, as a local event. Soldiers live, fight, and die within the immediate world of their battalion and the close circle of comrades, not

November 1943–November 1944

In November 1943, Roland Regan and the 348th Engineer Combat Battalion arrived in Liverpool, England aboard the recently refitted Liberty ship HMS *Mauretania*. Originally assigned to the First Army, they trained in various towns in England and Wales, spending most of this period in Swansea, Wales. There they trained as part of the preparations for the massive Allied D-Day invasion. In planning for D-Day, the 348th was attached to the 37th Engineers in support of the 16th Infantry Regiment. Under heavy German artillery fire Roland and Company A landed at the Easy Red sector of Omaha Beach between 9:30 and 10:30 A.M. of the first day of the invasion, June 6, 1944. Their mission was to construct roads leading from the beach to inland dump areas.[4] On June 18 they were transferred to the Fox White sector of Omaha Beach, where they unloaded over 300 LST and other craft as the Allies prepared to attack the German forces inland in France and Belgium.[5]

Throughout the summer and into early fall the 348th Engineers and Roland Regan worked on Omaha Beach unloading weapons, ammunition, and supplies for the advancing Allied forces. Through September 1944 the battalion had unloaded over 281,049 tons of supplies.[6] In October the battalion transferred to Arromanches to assist the British landing, which had fallen behind schedule. In gale force winds, rain, and mud, the men unloaded British ships, repaired supply roads, and engineered drainage. In late November the 348th was on the move again, this time to the port city of Cherbourg. Here they played a central role in the operation of the formerly Nazi-controlled "Terre Plein" dock. After clearing the harbor and port of sunken ships and German mines, the engineers unloaded Allied supplies for the push eastward. In Arromanches and Cherbourg Roland probably had his first personal encounter with the enemy. According to the battalion history, German prisoners of war assisted the men of the 348th in both beach operations. It was also during this time that Roland and his fellow engineers had time to experience French sites and cities. In early September some in his battalion visited the Palace of Versailles outside Paris and a few weeks later Roland himself visited the recently liberated "City of Light," Paris.

In October of 1944 Frederick Mauriello and the 309th Field Artillery Battalion arrived in England aboard the recently refitted *Carnavan Castle* troop ship.[7] Frederick had joined the battalion only that summer due to his required specialized radio training at the University of Connecticut. He was now one of two "fire direction" radio operators in the battalion's Headquarters Battery. The 309th was stationed in Bournemouth until it was rushed to join the Allied advance through France in November. On November 22, 1944, the battalion landed at the French port of Le Havre. Traveling with their tractor-drawn 155mm-howitzer artillery, the battalion marched and drove into Belgium, making final combat preparations in the towns of Mons and Hoeselt. In Hoeselt the men of the 309th saw their first German V-1 "Buzz Bomb" flying overhead.[8] During this time the battalion marched and sat in the same rain and mud as Roland's 348th Engineering Combat Battalion, which was also experiencing the infamous buzz bombs.[9] Roland and Frederick would not be this geographically close again until March of 1945. By then, each had seen some deadly serious combat.

December 1944–January 1945

For anyone familiar with the military history of World War II, the period from December 1944 through January 1945 had some of the heaviest fighting, and greatest casualties, for the U.S. Army during the entire war. This was the period of the Battle of the Ardennes Forest, better known as the Battle of the Bulge.

Roland and the 348th Engineering Combat Battalion began this dramatic period on the defensive. On the morning of December 16, the 5th and 6th SS Panzer Armies broke through into Luxembourg in a bold attempt to counterattack the Allied advance through France. The 348th

Engineers were reassigned for service as Combat Engineers and loaded trucks headed for Liège, Belgium, to support the First Army infantry, artillery, and armored units in their effort to counterattack the flanks of the German offensive.[10] Company A arrived in the vicinity of Namur, outside Liège, on Christmas Eve. That evening, as they attempted to sleep, German buzz bombs were "rattling along" overhead on their errands of destruction. In the cold, snow, and wind, the 348th arrived in Liège, only to find the city littered with glass and brick from buzz bombs that were being dropped every five minutes on average.[11] At Liège, they experienced the intensity and toll of the German attack, witnessing columns of wounded GIs pass through the city, and vehicles with bullet holes and smashed windshields. Company A headquartered at a chateau near Banneux and watched the vapor trails of the mounting air war over the Belgian city. The 348th was assigned to the 110th Engineer Group responsible for road maintenance and guarding dumps, bridges, and road obstacles just outside the city. Roland's Company A was the closest to the action among his battalion and they were under constant artillery fire until the German armies were halted only 20 miles southeast of Liège.[12]

While the 348th Engineering Combat Battalion was assigned to support troops holding Liège, Frederick and the 309th Field Artillery Battalion were fighting on the northernmost flank of "the Bulge." On December 11, 1944, the battalion crossed into Germany a few miles east of Roetgen on the edge of the Eupen Forest. There, in the cold and snow, the battalion readied its big guns for a massive artillery barrage in support of the 78th Division infantry attack on the German 272nd Ground Division, held up at the towns of Simmerath, Rollesbroich, Bickerath, and Kesternich.[13] On the morning of December 13 the battalion bombarded German positions and by nightfall all the towns but Kesternich were in the hands of U.S. forces. Kesternich would soon be captured, but at a high and bloody price.

Then came the German counterattack. In the cold gray morning of December 16, 1944, German General Karl von Rundstedt launched a desperate but mighty counteroffensive to halt the American advance and push U.S. forces back to the French coast. The German offensive, which lasted from December 16–27, was initially very successful. Frederick and the 309th were pinned down under heavy German artillery fire throughout the day and took many casualties. Between December 17 and 20 the Battle of the Bulge raged in the northern section. During these days the batteries of the 309th were firing over 300 rounds per hour at the advancing German forces.[14] By December 20 the battalion was forced back to Roetgen, where it supported the 78th Division's mission of stabilizing and defending the position against the expanding German attack on their southern flank. By late January the German offensive was over. Exhausted, without fuel and outnumbered, the German army became a defensive force once again. The 309th was soon on the move into Germany.

February 1945–April 1945

From late January to early April Roland and Frederick were both fighting in, around, or near water. In the final months of the war both the 348th and the 309th battled into Germany by traversing the swift currents and cold water of its numerous rivers and fighting the remnants of the retreating German army in every river town.

For Roland's Company A, the "river wars" were the defining experience of the war. The role that engineering combat battalions and engineering corps played during this crucial phase of the war cannot be overstated. These units built sturdy "Bailey" bridges, pontoon bridges, and treadways, shuttling troops across numerous rivers, almost always under a barrage of enemy artillery fire and strafing from the Luftwaffe. Without them the Allied advance would have ground to a halt.

Roland was in the thick of it. In the freezing cold of late January, Company A built a bridge for the advancing First Army at Salme-Chateau, Belgium, just outside Malmedy. Throughout February the battalion maintained hundreds of miles of roads deteriorating under the heavy traffic of infantry carriers, armor columns, and winter weather. They were now reclaiming some of the areas that they held during January, before the German offensive, and inching closer to Germany itself.[15]

By mid-February the Allied break in the German Siegfried Line was complete. Roland's engineering combat battalion was now both in high demand and in high gear, racing to traverse the rivers that lay between the U.S. armies and Berlin. On March 1 the 348th, headquartered near the German city of Düren, began to move toward the Rur (Roer) River. There they set about the dangerous job of clearing mines and repairing roads devastated by Allied and German artillery warfare. Roland and Company A built a timber-bent bridge across the Rur in Düren and re-modeled a hospital building.[16] In early March Company A built three 44-foot spans across the Rur River. With the stunning Allied crossing of the Rhine River at Remagen on March 9, the 348th moved south to Net-tersheim and then to Königsfeld. There they continued road mainte-nance and salvaged government equipment and material in the sector.[17]

In April Roland took part in the campaigns to cross the Ruhr, Sieg, and Elbe Rivers. These rivers were the final obstacles outside of Berlin and the last defense of the Third Reich. On April 11th, Roland and Company A were dispatched to Siegburg just outside Bonn. There they constructed two bridges across the Sieg River, removing mines as they went. On April 30th they moved to Dahlen, near the Elbe River. In a dramatic moment, Roland and his company assisted the fabled 82nd

Airborne Division in their attack across the Elbe near Bleckede. Throughout the day on the 30th they ferried troops across the Elbe as German artillery shells whizzed overhead, exploding in the water and on the banks of the river. For the 348th, the war was far from over.[18]

Throughout this time in Düren and Siegburg, the 348th were busy taking and guarding German prisoners, who were now surren-dering in droves. Roland witnessed the cost of war on the civilian pop-ulation as tens of thousands of German civilians in cars, trucks, wagons, bicycles, and on foot flooded through the city in a human ex-odus. Throughout April Roland watched as thousands of Russian, Polish, and Italian slave laborers, liberated from war plants, migrated in search of food, shelter, and security.[19]

Frederick and the 309th Field Artillery Battalion were also waging river war. After their hard fighting during the Battle of the Bulge, the battalion moved with the 78th Division to break through the Siegfried Line and capture the Rur River dams intact. The dams, specifically the Schwammenauel Dam, which held back some 22 billion gallons of water, were in enemy hands and if blown could submerge and destroy all the towns along the Rur from Heimbach to Doermund.[20] Beginning on January 30, the 309th provided tremendous artillery barrages to support the recapturing of towns lost to the German Bulge counter-offensive earlier in the month. Frederick directed fire from his position atop a church steeple, town by town, as infantry battalions beat back the Germans. On February 12 the prime objective, the Schwammenauel Dam, was taken intact after a surprise attack.

As with the 348th, the greatest challenges of the river war lay ahead with the 309th's crossing of the heavily defended rivers in the Rhine and Ruhr valleys. By mid-March the battalion and its artillery were involved in the bloody battle for the Remagen Bridge as well as other crossing points on the Rhine. On March 21 elements of the

309th crossed the Remagen Bridge under heavy fire, including strafing from Messerschmitt Me 262 and Arado Ar 234, the first operational jet fighter and jet bomber respectively.[21] With the bridges over the Rhine secured, the 309th and the 78th Division were set to push toward Berlin.

May 1945–August 1945

After the successful crossings of Germany's main rivers, Roland's and Frederick's battalions pushed rapidly east into the heart of the Third Reich. During this time Allied soldiers entered into the bombed towns east of the Rhine and witnessed the devastation that the war wreaked on the lives and property of civilians, including the elderly, women, and children. While there was serious fighting from pockets of German resistance, late April through the summer of 1945 was a period for much reflection about the war and the costs of war.

Roland and the 348th took part in the long-awaited meeting of the U.S. and Soviet armies in early May at the Elbe River. At last allies could shake hands over a defeated Nazi Germany. On May 3 the battalion oversaw the surrender of the entire German 21st Army to the American and Soviet armies near Ludwigslust. Company A ferried U.S. and Red Army soldiers as well as German prisoners back and forth across the Elbe River and directed traffic on the bridges they had constructed.[22]

It was near Ludwigslust that Roland witnessed the horrors of the Holocaust. There he entered the gates of the Wöbbelin concentration camp just outside the German town of Ludwigslust. Here Roland photographed the results of the Nazi quest to create a racially purified "New Germany." In the words of the battalion history and supported by later research, "The Commanding General of the 82nd Airborne Division (General James Gavin) ordered two hundred families of the city of Ludwigslust to obtain one body each from a common grave at the camp to transport and bury the bodies in a cemetery prepared in the center of town. The orders were carried out."[23] Throughout April and May Allied forces on the eastern and western fronts were liberating concentration and death camps, witnessing, with Roland and his comrades, this encounter with inhumanity and death.

On May 7 the German military signed an unconditional surrender, which ended the war in Europe. Like many units, the men of the 348th received the news with a mixture of reserve and muted enthusiasm. The memories of lost friends during the war and anxieties about being sent to the Pacific Theater limited the celebration. So did the realities of occupation. By late May and early June 1945 the battalion was on the move again. On May 23 they were ordered to move to a former German Luftwaffe airfield near Waggum outside Braunschweig. On June 19 they were alerted of a move to Dessau and ultimately Berlin via the famous German Autobahn—the superhighway constructed by the Nazis. So began a period of comical confusing orders know to the men of the battalion as "The Battle of the Autobahn."[24] By the end of June, the 348th Engineering Combat Battalion was breaking up. Roland, like millions of other soldiers, began moving back west, fearing, and expecting, to begin a second tour of duty in the Pacific. Fortunately that never happened. On August 14, 1945, after two devastating atomic bombs, Japan surrendered and Roland was headed back to Boston.

As April began Frederick and the 309th moved northeast across the Autobahn. Their mission was to help clean out the "Ruhr Pocket" in the junction between the First and Ninth Armies. On April 4 they pushed northeast toward the Sieg River with the ultimate aim of occupying the industrial city of Essen. All along the way German troops surrendered to the advancing battalion. In Remscheid, the 16th German Panzer Corps surrendered en masse. On May 8 news of Germany's surrender reached the 309th while they were in Dillenburg.[25]

Like Roland, Frederick feared and expected to be transferred to the Pacific Theater. On May 12 he and his battalion moved to Kassel, a northern city in the "security control zone" of the 78th Division. Frederick was now part of the Allied occupation of Germany. There he pulled the best guard duty: guarding an abandoned German brewery. On July 9th the battalion moved to the towns of Kassel and Niederelsungen to begin training exercises for service in the Pacific. It was there that they learned of the Japanese surrender. Frederick remained in Europe as part of the Allied occupation force until early 1946 when he was honorably discharged and returned to Boston.

Journey through World War II in Images and Words

What follows is a documentary history of Roland Regan's and Frederick Mauriello's journeys through World War II. Roland's photographs are chronologically arranged to correspond with Frederick's letters (transcribed, with some examples of the originals) as they moved through Europe during 1944 and 1945. The juxtaposition of the photographs and the letters provides a unique combination of images and words not possible if published separately. Roland's photographs provide a visual representation of Frederick's words, which in turn provide a voice for Roland's images. Importantly, the photographs and letters are arranged to present a parallel journey through World War II, not a historically identical one. The photographs are not representations of Frederick's exact experiences recounted in the letters, but separate images correlated to those experiences.

The above histories of the 348th Engineering Combat Battalion and the 309th Field Artillery Battalion provide the context and timeline for this extraordinary documentary story. While we have written a brief section introducing specific photographs and letters for each chapter, and inserted captions for each photograph and letter included, we hope that the images and words speak for themselves.

Notes

1. Stephen Ambrose, *Citizen Soldiers* (New York: Touchstone Books, 1998).
2. Keith Bryan, *Pack Up and Move: A Pictorial History of the 348th Engineer Combat Battalion* (Columbus, Nebraska: The Art Printery, n.d.).
3. *The 309th Field Artillery Battalion: World War II European Theatre of Operations* (Privately printed at the Rumford Press, 1947.)
4. Keith Bryan, *Pack Up and Move*, p. 36.
5. Ibid., pp. 39–40.
6. Ibid., p. 55.
7. *The 309th Field Artillery Battalion*, pp. 18–20.
8. Ibid., pp. 22–25.
9. Keith Bryan, *Pack Up and Move*, p. 66.
10. Ibid.
11. Ibid., pp. 66–67.
12. Ibid., pp. 67–68.
13. *The 309th Field Artillery Battalion*, pp. 28–29.
14. Ibid., p. 33.
15. Keith Bryan, *Pack Up and Move*, pp. 74–76.
16. Ibid., p. 78.
17. Ibid., p. 84.
18. Ibid., p. 89

19. Ibid., pp. 85–86.

20. "The Story of the 78th Lightning Division" (Paris: Curial-Artchereau, 1945), p. 5.

21. Ibid., p. 10; and *The 309th Field Artillery Battalion*, p. 50.

22. Keith Bryan, *Pack Up and Move*, pp. 88–90.

23. Ibid., p. 92. For a more extensive description of the liberation of the Wöbbelin concentration camp by the Allies in April–May 1945, see Robert H. Abzug, *Inside the Vicious Heart: Americans and the Liberation of Nazi Concentration Camps* (New York and Oxford: Oxford University Press, 1985), pp. 63–73.

24. Keith Bryan, *Pack Up and Move*, p. 96.

25. *The 309th Field Artillery Battalion*, p. 56.

Chapter One

The Journey Begins

(April 1943–May 1944)

LIKE ALL SOLDIERS, Roland and Frederick began their military service by training for war. In Roland's case this meant grueling training routines with the 348th Combat Engineers in both the United States and Great Britain. The first photographs of the collection capture Roland and the men of the 348th in their first overseas training site, Camp Manselton outside Swansea, Wales. At Camp Manselton and later on the Swansea seacoast, the 348th carried out practice operations unloading men, ammunition, and supplies for the imminent invasion of the Continent. The photographs capture the sense of excitement and playfulness of the GIs, many of them overseas for the first time. They show the important sense of camaraderie and friendships developing among Company A. This sense of togetherness would serve the 348th well when they hit the beaches of Normandy. The photographs also give a sense of the military preparations themselves. They include shots of a P-38 Lightning and a B-17 Flying Fortress in the days immediately before they flew in to support the D-Day landings and of field artillery to be loaded on the massive landing craft.

The first letters from the collection, written during Frederick's training at Camp Forrest, Tennessee, and the University of Alabama, relate his thoughts and emotions about the army, service to country, and of course, the separation from his family back in Boston. The letters capture the primitive physical conditions experienced during field training and the eternal soldier's quest for leave. More importantly, the letters introduce some powerful themes that run throughout the collection. In a letter dated Easter, April 25, 1943, Frederick contemplates the central importance of his mother and the Catholic faith in his and his family's life. At one point he compares his mother to the Virgin Mary sending off a son to be sacrificed, but ends on a note of humility, "My sacrifice of being away from home for a period seems minute and insincere." In a letter to his sister Marie he writes about the quality and intelligence of the citizen-soldiers that surround them. These are not professional soldiers, but researchers, curators at zoos, chemical engineers, and medical students. In the final letter of this chapter Frederick reflects, during a Memorial Day service, on the possibility of death

Settling in: The photograph on page 15 shows Roland standing in front of the 348th Engineering Combat Battalion HQ at Camp Manselton outside Swansea, Wales, in November 1943. He had many photos taken of himself, which he then sent home to let his family know how he was faring.

during wartime. He is struck by the fact that none of the men with him thought they could be killed in war, while they accepted that others would be. In fact, many of the men standing with him that day would be memorialized a year later after the battalion saw combat in the European Theater.

~

Pvt (still) Mauriello
H.Q BTRY 208 F.A.G.
Camp Forrest
You Know Where
3/11/43

Dear Ma

We have just come back from the field. Gee but its nice out there. Spring has arrived here, the green grass has broken through the resisting ground and the bare trees are dressing for the vital summer to camp. During the day the temperature rises to 70 and at night it becomes very cool.

In our pup tents we have to share blankets. We with 2 blankets under us and 4 blankets over us are quite sufficient to block out the cold. As far as washing and shaving go, we are still very primitive. We wash and shave out of the river. Gee you dont know how good Boston water is till you leave it. The water here can not be made into suds. You dont shave the hair off your face; instead you pull it off.

Personally I would rather be out on the field than in this hole. Out on the field we do nothing but radio work and an occasional turn of guard duty. While here we do nothing but K.P., Guard duty and inspections. Tommorow we have K.P again.

The reason why we do K.P, washing trucks and etc. is this is a national guard outfit that has been down here 2 years and back home together about the same time. Out of 84 men only 21 men are not rated. The 21 men being recruits, us, and since we havn't any ratings, we have to do all the work.

Members of the 348th, Company A, on the move in Wales.

They have my name up at the office as going to radio school for 1½ months. Do you know in 6 weeks they have let me go to school 6 hours. Just because one of the seargents don't want to go, I cant go.

There is some hope though. My name has been turned in and approved by Regimental head quarters for me to go to college under the government specialized training program. So unless something happens between here and Washington I will go to school. Don't pin your hopes too much on it; because I know better than that. If it don't go through I am going to put in for a transfer.

Well I suppose I might as well tell you. I was suppose to come home next tuesday on my Easter furlough. I was promised to be sent home on April 20 by the battary commander. Some of the old fellows here who work up at the office didn't like the idea. So when the list went up to the office instead of an old man and new man going, it turned out that the top seargent and one of the office boys went. Even my radio seargent was cheated out of his furlough by the office clique. Soon as my transfer comes through or my orders to go to school come through I am going to look up a couple of the boys who think they are smart; but until then I am going to keep battling for April 20. Even though I know it is hopeless.

My mail is coming through all Right. I have got letters from everybody and a package from Neddy (dates). Hold up on the package & readers digest, I haven't even read January's yet.

I'm making the novena every Midnight to the blessed Virgin; and I also go to Mass everyday while I am in camp.

Thats all for now ROGER OVER

Love Freddy

~

Roland with other members of Company A in Wales. These young men, from all walks of life, trained together and were to experience war together. Theirs was a unique generation.

As was the case with many young GIs, the church played an important role for Roland and Frederick. Roland attended services in Wales on Christmas in 1943 and took this photograph. It was probably his first Christmas away from home, and the service would have helped him feel connected to his family.

Pvt Mauriello
H.Q BTRY 208 F.A.G
Camp Forrest Tennessee
April 25, 1943

Dear Edna,

Today is Easter, the first Easter I have been separated from my family. I am a little bit sad. Sad but not for me. I am sad for Ma's sake. I all ways can enjoy myself no matter where I am, and always laugh at every day occurrences. I am as flexeable as I am expendable; But not Ma. Her ideals are cemented. Her work is fixed. Her work, her life, her past, present and future is us. It is for us she lives for. She has settled her mind into being the best mother in the world. In this task she has notably succeeded. I believe she is the best mother in the world. You must believe in that. It is the duty of every child to believe that his is the best mother in the world; but we can say this without any qualms of conscience, for Ma has proved that she is willing to make any sacrifice for us.

Even though I am many miles away from Home I know what is happening home. As it is to us, it is all over the world. Millions of families are uniting at church to pray for those who are called to sacrifice their lives, just as He was asked to lay down his life 1900 years ago for peace to descend over the world.

We can pray for peace. The best we can pray for is a just peace. Peace can not be obtained until complete victory is achieved.

I know Ma. She went to church, prayed for the unification of her family, came home and cooked a meal that can not be matched. Just before meal serving, she looked around and saw her family was not all there. Ma probably cried. The food has no taste to her.

It is up to you to console her. It is from our Virgin Mother you must draw for courage and example. It is from the scene on the mount, that you can draw courage to steel yourself and carry on. For she lost a son to a cause in which He believed in. Our Virgin Mother lost more than her son's presence. She saw him lose his life. That is the greatest sacrifice man can make. My sacrifice of being away from home for a period seems minute and insincere.

You must take faith and hope from the scripture. When He said "In a little while you will not see me. And in a while you shall see me."

I do not profess to know what a period of time is a "little while". But you must believe me when I say that no matter how long the time or how great the distance between us, I shall try to live up to your expectations of me; and at all times I will conduct myself as a good Catholic and a good soldier.

Sending you a sincere Easter Greetings. I remain your loving brother

Freddy.

Roland's 348th Combat Engineering Battalion portrait, taken in England in March 1944, shows his serious side as he contemplates the road ahead.

May 30, 1944

Dear Marie,

I received your over due letter. Thats a pretty good record. Three letters in 3 weeks. I suppose I could write that same line for years before it makes an impression. Yes! I got that money order weeks ago I just havent had a chance to cash it.

Today we stopped all activities for 2 hours in the morning. We had memorial services for all the men who were killed in the battles of this division of World war one, and services for all the boys who left this division and were killed at the Anglo Beachead, just below Rome.

The services were very impressive. I am enclosing the program.

Its funny; but today's gathering had a physcoligical twist to it. There were thousands of fellows there. Everyone felt sorry for the boys there. Each soldier knew that out of that gathering there, there would be hundreds and maybe thousands of the boys would be killed before next Memorial day; but each soldier wasn't afraid because they knew they were the one that was going to come back. Not one boy admitted that they thought they were going to be casualties; but each predicted that a large percentage of the boys would become casualties. I guess that represents the conceit of each human being.

The volley of shots fired and the sound of the bugle playing Taps left the boys with chills.

We went to the Movies last night and saw "2 girls and a sailor". It was terrific. The boys really whistled and laughed through it all

Thats all for now

Freddie

~

Pvt Mauriello
Co. C ATO House
S.C.U No 3414 Star
University Alab.
June 43

Dear Dot

Life still moves serenely at the country club. We are having supervised study until we get shipped out.

What an assortment of characters we have collected here. Never in the history of American education has there been enrolled in any school. First I must say this is one of the most brilliant groups ever gathered. Every man here unlike the average college class has been through the road of life. They were "prepped" not at Groton or St Marks; but out in the noisy den of industry, the nerve wracking task of medicine, the [illegible word] of the business world and toughened out in the army maneuver areas, where you sleep on the ground and act as if time was pushed back several centuries.

We are a hard bitter lot. We have been formally schooled at some of the best universities, became cogs in our enormous industries and made and spent thousands of dollars.

The business of war: Artillery and trucks being prepared for the imminent D-Day invasion.

Take the boys around me for examples. There is Al, the boy who shares the upper half of our doubledecker bunk. Before the war he held an important position in Washington with the signal corp. Bob, the boy who sleeps beside me, is recognized as one of the best authorities on reptiologey, study of snakes. He was assistant curator for the Philadelphia Zoo, the largest zoo in the world. He has had newspaper interviews, and has been interviewed over the radio with Lily Pons. He knows Frank Buck personally and calls hundreds of people in the public limelight by their first names.

There is the "Greek". A boy who studied at some of the best universities of Europe. He was studying at one of the Greek universities when the Germans came and had to flee the country just ahead of the German Panzer units. To him Revenge is a personal thing.

There's Press the chemical engineer, still laughing at the world, Babcock graduate of our best prep school. Red, a third year student in Medical School. There is more.

A hard tough group that laugh at glamour cadets, stare at the coeds; but in all the parades all brought here by a realistic government to do the dirty work after the war. Theres no glamour here, just the will to make good and hate.

Love Freddie

A B-17G Flying Fortress in southern England weeks before Operation Overlord commences. This Boeing aircraft, with its characteristic profile, was widely used as a heavy bomber in both the European and Pacific Theaters. It carried a crew of nine men and a maximum 12,000-pound bomb load.

(Wondering Whats It All About) Pvt Mauriello
Etc
Etc
Etc
United States of Alabama
June 18, 1943 1/2 A.D

Dear Marie,

The temperature has now dropped to a comfortable 97 degrees. It wasn't bad last night though it dropped to a cool eighty. Last night was the first night in three weeks that I could sleep. I say could sleep; because sleep could be had if we had peace. Peace was not to be had.

I was sleeping comfortably, dreaming peacefull dreams of a private, like jamming whistles down seargents throats and giving hot foots to second lieutenants when, whango, a rat runs up the back of my neck over my head down my face across my throat & down the other side. I jumped up. I don't mind rattle snakes that sleep under blankets with you. I don't mind red ants that eat your packages before the mailman even delivers it to you; but I do object to the rats who wear shoes down here and kick you in the face as they run by.

I calmed down after a while and went back to sleep. Clumpty clump, another one ran over, then another. I thought I was lying down in the middle of a race track. Maybe I was in the way of the rat races that the high school jitterbugs talk about. That bed had more rats running around it than there are ladies running down Filene's basement during dollar day.

After a couple of hours of this I retreated to the other end of the bed where there was nothing but dive bombing mosquitos. This morning I woke up to look at my barracks bag. I found out that the cute little devils had eaten 2 pairs of my summer pants, 2 pairs of socks and a towel. The night cost me about 10 dollars.

About 2 AM the rats departed and I got back to sleep again. In comes the boy who sleeps in the upper bunk. He was supposed to be in at 10. He shakes me awake; and I see this happy crazy face with dreamy eyes. I said "What in heavens name do you want at 2 o'clock in the morning. Anyone with brains would be sleeping." He ignores my compliment, and says "Red, I was out with Trudi." I said, "You bum, is that what you wake me out of the arms of Morpheous for. You were out with a girl, so what." He looks at me, his big foolish blue eyes all alight and says "I kissed her." Again I said, "So what does that make me a general?" The foolish soldier comes back with "Your jealous! You have talked to her three hours every Sunday for the last two Sundays and couldn't even get a

"An assortment of characters": Rocky Marciano (left) with Roland and a fellow 348th Combat Engineer. Like Frederick and Roland, Marciano came from an immigrant family in the Boston area. He got his start boxing in amateur tournaments at Fort Lewis.

date" I answered "I'm not particular who I talk to. Someone has to keep up the hostesses morale." "What do you mean you tramp?" he yells back at me. "Your not particular who you are talking to. Your talking about the girl I love. I demand an apology." I rolled over, and said "Nuts." He grabs me by the shoulder and says "Come on out and fight you coward. You aren't going to talk about my girl that way."

By this time the rest of the ward is awaken yelling "Quiet you bums, we want to sleep! Break his neck and shut him up." Then the shoes start flying in our direction. In five minutes we have enough shoes to set up a shoe business and collect no. 17 stamps.

I am intelligent so I decide discretion is the better part of valor so I apologize. We are now bosom buddies again. This goes on every night with a different girl's name being mentioned.

By gosh if the army fights the Axisis as hard as we do each other over girls we will be home by Christmas.

Lots of Love and laughs

Freddie

P.S. Hold up on the mail. Im on the move again. Going to another school

Roland horses around atop a P-38 Lightning in April 1944.

Chapter Two

Invasion!
D-Day and War in the European Theatre

(June 1944–November 1944)

THE MONTHS OF PREPARATION in the United States and England could not have prepared Roland and Frederick for the ferocity that they would face fighting the German armies in Europe in the coming months. For Roland and the 348th, the baptism of fire was the Allied landings at Normandy, France, known to history as D-Day. The 348th landed on Omaha Beach on June 6, 1944. While they did not experience the ferocious combat on the beaches that the first wave of Allied soldiers did, Roland witnessed the immediate aftermath and devastation of the largest invasion in history. The photographs that follow represent his first experiences of the human and material costs of war. Images of the wasted hulls of landing craft on the now calm rocky shoreline poignantly contrast the violence of war against a natural setting. For Roland such scenes must have also engendered a great deal of awe and anxiety about the future. Here were landing craft that he had trained in, and packed with equipment, after their immersion in the crucible of war. Other photos capture the sense of being a

part of this incredible moment in history. In one, Roland shows men and machines disembarking on the beaches, illustrating the incredible logistics of moving whole armies ashore in a matter of weeks. Another photo proudly documents the capture of a mighty German shore fortification by the Allies.

But Roland is also sensitive to the human side of D-Day. He chooses to photograph two officers relaxing and talking on the beach. He also remembers the dead. He takes time to photograph a fresh cemetery for GIs who have been killed storming the beaches.

Roland and the 348th, however, were too busy to dwell on the devastation as they began to build and repair roads for the Allied push through France toward Berlin. Like all soldiers Roland relished his leave, which gave this boy from Lynn, Massachusetts, an opportunity to sample the "City of Light," Paris. His photographs represent the everyday experiences and interests of the GI away from combat. Roland visits a Paris café and shops in the city bazaar. Interestingly, Roland

D-Day+4, June 1944, Omaha Beach, Easy Red (landing site), U.S. 1st Army, 348th Combat Engineering Battalion, Company A, arrives in Normandy. The 348th played an essential role in unloading ordinance and supplies for the Allies. They also repaired damaged roads and cleared others as the Allies moved further inland.

Home of the brave: Many of the fallen Allied soldiers were buried in cemeteries such as this one.

turns the camera over to a friend to have his photograph taken in front of a sign at the railway station of the French town Chateau-Thierry—the site of the famous World War I battle that cost thousands of American lives. Clearly the historic significance of American soldiers once again fighting on European soil was not lost on Roland.

Paris is where the letters of Frederick Mauriello begin to correspond closely with the photographs of Roland Regan. Frederick's October 26, 1944, letter from Paris to his parents back in Revere, Massachusetts, put into words the images of Roland's Paris photographs. In this playful letter he relates the excitement and novelty of Paris. He is struck by the stores, the new fashions and styles, and especially the brightly colored hair of the Parisian women. A major theme of the entire collection of letters emerges here. Frederick's point of reference is Boston, the only cosmopolitan world he had experienced up to 1944. Europe and its inhabitants are always compared to Boston and Bostonians. Clearly this is an at-

tempt to relate his new experiences in familiar terms to his parents and sisters in the States. It also reveals the sense of adventure that Frederick felt in going over-seas for the first time. Like Roland, Frederick is in many ways a parochial young man experiencing the cosmopolitan culture of Europe for the first time.

However, like the 348th, Frederick and the 309th Field Artillery Battalion experienced the devastation of war during this period. Frederick and his battalion entered the European Theater of Operations through the French port of Le Havre on November 22, 1944. As his letters from November and December 1944 document, they entered France and then Belgium as libera-tors. Like Roland, Frederick was struck by the destruction and dislocation of war and, in this case, German occupation. His war is physical, and the scenes of men and machine mired in mud dominate his narration home to his sisters and parents. He was also touched by the generosity of the common people who gave them their homes and barns to sleep in despite having suffered almost three years of German occupation. A powerful theme that runs throughout the letters—the cost of war to the common people, especially children—emerges.

For Frederick and the 309th this tranquil Belgian scene was to be shattered only weeks later by the advancing German troops at the Battle of the Bulge.

(Above) **D-Day+4, June 1944, Omaha Beach, Fox White.** *Men of the 348th Combat Engineering Battalion find a brief moment to relax as the Allies prepare for the big push.*

~

October 26, Paris.

Dear Folks,

Its true what they say about Paris. Everything that you have ever heard is true. Its strictly out of this world. I have never seen a city so beautiful. Its an oasis

(Top left) D-Day+15, June 1944, Omaha Beach bluffs, where the 348th Combat Engineering Battalion prepares to destroy a German cannon installation.

(Top right) D-Day+16, June 1944, Omaha Beach. A damaged U.S. invasion craft is left abandoned after the storms of June 17–21. This craft was eventually removed by the 348th Combat Engineering Battalion.

(Right) Roland is thinking of World War I as he has himself photographed at the train station at Chateau-Thierry in late September or October 1944. Chateau-Thierry would come to be displaced in the public memory by such epic struggles as the Battle of the Bulge (see chapter 3).

of beauty in a desert of Destruction. Every large city in Europe is devastated except this one.

I have missed one train out of this city. The average soldier misses Four trains. There is a hurricane on the English Channel. I'm praying it holds up shipping for a few days so I can stay here.

There are thousands of stores. They are even more wonderful than the ones we have in the states. There are more stores than you would think. The number of stores is out of proportion to the size of the city. Its like Tremont Street; but extending for miles. Every other store is a perfume store. The other stores are luxury stores selling Furcoats and jewelry. There isn't another type store except night clubs.

The women are beautiful; but in my opinion overrated by the boys. They use too much makeup. Everyone goes through the streets as if they were going to a big dance. Their hair styles are beautifully set. Their clothes are wonderfully designed years ahead of ours. They really have some styles. I'm impressed by the hair coloring. Its really funny. The style is Red hair. All the girls are wearing Red hair Except for a few blondes, and girls with <u>BLUE HAIR</u>. At one time last spring, the style was BLUE hair. Its a bluish gray but it doesn't appeal to me.

I like walking the streets walking past the stores. The perfume smell is everywhere. This is the home of all the labels you see in perfume labels. I priced some perfume. 100 dollars an ounce for some.

I have visited many beautiful Cathederals. Notre Dame etc. The enclosed postcards are of my favorite. The Church of Madeleine. Thats all for now.

Love Freddie

~

November 15, 1944

Dear Marie,

Today the mail caught up with me. I received 2 regular letters dated the 16th and 18th. I received your's and Edna's letter of November second and fourth. I

(Right) Despite some scarcity of goods in wartime France, our boys were amazed at what Paris had to offer. Here Roland shops at an open market during his leave in late September 1944.

(Below) Small world: Hometown boys Roland and Chet Whitten run into each other in France in September 1944. Their story in the newspaper was welcome relief from the often heartbreaking reports from the front.

OLD CHUMS MEET IN FRANCE

Private Roland J. Regan, 21, son of Mrs. Margaret M. Regan, 291A Broadway, and the late Patrick J. Regan, recently met his chum, Private C. R. Whitten, 21, son of C. G. Whitten, 100 Den Quarry road, in France, where both are stationed with Combat Engineer units. Privates Regan and Whitten went to Pickering Junior High and English High school together, entered the Army only a few days apart 17 months ago. Regan went overseas in November, 1943, while Whitten crossed the Atlantic in June. They met in France, discovering that their units were stationed only a mile apart.

also received a package from Big Lucy. Today we went on a detail. We didn't work too much. Most of our energy was expended in dodging the children. I felt sorry for them so I gave them some hard candy about 7 pieces. That was a mistake. there was a riot around here. All the kids grabbed my clothes. Then the rest of the day I was besieged by the kids. I was the soldier who was supposed to have pocketfuls of candy. These kids haven't had candy for years.

Love Freddi

~

Somewhere in France
Thanksgiving 44

Dear Pa,

Im now in France. The weather continues to be cold and damp. It hasn't been completly sunny for one day since we hit Europe. Everything is a sea of mud. There is still a lot to be thankfull for this day. I have my health, excellent spirits, Faith in God and have the finest parents and sisters in the world all intact. I have no worry's about the future. I have faith, prayer and the finest army with me. I shall see this through. The way home is through Berlin. So every mile we move foreward is a step nearer home.

Love Freddie

~

Somewhere in Belgium
November 28, 1944

Dear Marie,

We are really racing across Borders. You don't know how lucky you are in the U.S. to escape the ravishes of war. The sight of whole villages leveled and deserted has a depressing effect. The roads are lined with twisted masses of steel that were once tanks and trucks.

We got a warm feeling when all the population of the large towns came out to greet us and wave their hands. They stood until late at night cheering us on. You should see how grateful the children were for a piece of hard candy. The most grateful people are Belgium People. They want to give us everything the Germans left them. They insist on us going into their homes. More tomorrow

Love Freddy

~

November 30, 1943 [sic]

Dear Edna,

I'm now feeling that I'm finally worth my $60. It gave you a warm pleasant feeling inside receiving the waves and kisses blown at you by the French population as we rode by. The French countryside was beautiful where the war bypassed it. It looked ugly and mournful where the battle was fought. It gave one an eerie feeling to go through towns, completely boarded up and deserted. When we passed through an inhabited town, People all came out and waved. The girls were extremely well dressed. Reports from the boys who went to Paris. They are extremely well dressed and look more chick than our girls. They live in splendor; but food and cigarettes are scarce. Cigarettes go for $6 a pack. Chocklate bars go a long way in bargaining.

It was in Belgium where we received our best treatment. The people insist on giving us everything they have. They really have nothing. On a road march we stopped near this farm. We asked the lady if we could sleep in her barn. Barn nothing! She insisted we sleep in her house. They offered us everything. The family put 20 soldiers up for the night and refused to take a cent. We chipped in cigarettes and a few crackers left from our K ration. They were overwhelmed.

As we went on, regardless of the time of night people came out of their houses, and during our halt they gave us cider, beer and apples.

Roland (left) and a fellow 348th Combat Engineer outside Paris in late September 1944. Most of these young men had never been abroad before, and enjoying the sights together was a high point of their leave.

Enjoying his leave in the authentic Parisian manner, Roland relaxes and people-watches in an outdoor café. Note the broken window to the left.

The girls and children are beautiful and also very polite. They will wait patiently at the end of our chow lines and take our left over food and thank us. There is no shoving. All the people use our used coffee grounds. At one place a lady scraped them off the field where we threw them.

We are sleeping in a barn of an old Chateau. I have my bed roll on top of a hay pile 10 feet high its really better than a feather bed.

Mail is pretty slow I have received two letters and your package. The other mail that trickles through is Camp Pickett mail of OCT 14th. Make sure its addressed correctly. You and Gerry send my mail through the Navy Channels. Maybe its a good idea; because thats the only mail I have received. [In the original, this paragraph is circled by a censor; see page 36.]

Tonight I am writing this letter in a small cafe. There is a cafe or Pub every ten doors in Europe. It's a small wall papered room with a bar at one end. There is an accordionist up in one corner playing classical pieces. He has just finished a medley of American songs and Christmas Carols in which all the soldiers have just joined in the singing. After playing and singing Silent Night. We were all very quiet and had a lump in our throats. So long for now and Merry Christmas if you don't hear from me for awhile.

Love Freddy

Chapter Three

The Battle of the Bulge

(December 1944–February 1945)

Lᴏᴏᴋ ᴍᴀɴʏ Aᴍᴇʀɪᴄᴀɴ sᴏʟᴅɪᴇʀs Roland and Frederick saw their most intense combat from November 1944 through February 1945 during the "Battle of the Bulge." Roland and the 348th Engineer Combat Battalion spent most of this period in and around Liège, Belgium. Here Company A was under constant German artillery and rocket fire as they guarded and repaired the bridges and roads into Liège. The photographs from this period reflect the aftermath of the fierce German attack and Allied counterattack. Early photographs document the 348th in combat uniforms as they march through Belgium. Later photographs document destroyed German Tiger tanks left behind as the Allies advanced through Belgium into Germany. One powerful photograph captures a defeated German soldier surrendering to a member of the 348th. The expression on this soldier's face tells the story of the turning of the tide of war as the German Army began its slow retreat back to Berlin.

Frederick and the 309th Field Artillery Battalion spent December 1944 and January 1945 in the thick of the northernmost flank of the Bulge. Frederick directed artillery fire in support of the 78th Division infantry attack on the German occupied towns of Simmerath, Rollesbroich, Bickerath, and Kesternich. He saw his most intense fighting of the war, retreating and then retaking towns street by street. The letters from this period illustrate, from a very personal perspective, the thoughts and emotions of an ordinary man seeing violent combat for the first time. In an extraordinary series of touching and humorous letters, he relates his friendship with a three-year old Belgian girl called Markie. He befriends her, walks guard duty with her, and even has a run-in with a colonel because of her. It reveals the human side of war and the personality of the man. Freddie is a soldier and a liberator, but he is still a big brother missing his sisters at home and wanting to protect the innocent.

But big brothers also have to be soldiers, and the letters from mid-December 1944 through January 1945 strike a more serious and somewhat sad tone. Frederick is clearly in battle daily and on December 23 writes, "Today for the first time in a month I changed under-

Roland's photo here, and Roland atop a tank on the previous page show remnants of the Battle of the Bulge: destroyed German Mark V (Tiger) tanks in Belgium in January 1945. This legendary weapon, with its 88-mm gun and armour up to 110 mm thick, was ultimately defeated by the Allies' determination, so aptly expressed in Frederick's letters.

wear." A poignant letter on Christmas Eve 1944 relates his and his fellow soldiers' sense of homesickness as they spend the holidays in a bomb shelter listening to Christmas songs over the radio. Interestingly, the military censors circle for editing a line relating that the boys cried listening to Bing Crosby's "White Christmas." Any evidence of demoralization was considered dangerous by the military authorities. By January 1945 Frederick is reflecting on the costs of war as he witnesses civilian casualties and destruction of civilian homes. In a moving letter to his mother on January 28 he obviously fears for his life and ends the letter, "I just like to say is pray hard, your as near to God as any person is."

~

Somewhere in Belgium
December 3, 1944

Hi Dot,

Today I received a large batch of mail, including your letters of Nov 20, 22, about the Dances. Well chicken I got myself a little Belgian Girl Friend. A very nice brunette. I went walking with her last night and this morning. She's really a good looker. Relax my girl MARKIE is three. While walking guard, she came out of her house and held on to my hand and walked with me. After a while I gave her a piece of chocklate. She went wild with joy. I had quite a job to make her go home. This morning at seven when I went on shift Markie grabbed my hand and off we marched to our post. It was quite a sight me a big soldier with a gun in one hand holding hands with a three year old walking guard at attention.

Love Freddy

~

Somewhere in Belgium

December 4, 1944

Dear Marie,

Everything is still going fine. My little girl MARKIE is making me trouble. She insists on walking guard with me. Yesterday when I walked she was holding my hand and walking with me when the colonel came by. He looked at me queerly but started walking by. All of a sudden MARKIE grabbed him by pistol and started pulling him towards me. She wanted the colonel to walk with us. He looked at me with a glare. I turned red and smiled weakly. I try to make Markie leave go; but she insisted on the old boy walking with us. Finally I broke her grip on the C.O. and walked down the road whistling with MARKIE holding on my hand and walking as fast as her little legs would carry her. Later I told Markie off. Its just as well that she doesn't understand English.

Love Freddie

Both Frederick and Roland experienced real hospitality from the grateful liberated Belgians. Here Roland is pictured with a Belgian family in Chênée, outside of Liège, in February.

December 22, 1944

Dear Dot,

Everything is still under control. Life keeps on going its gay-way. We have improved on comforts. We have ourselves a radio. For the first time in months we heard music. You should have seen the boys gather around the radio! Just like little kids around a Christmas Tree, Christmas morn. When we heard Dinah Shore sing "Now I Know." When she finished singing the boys were silent. There was more than one lump in the throat in the group. We don't want bonuses or medals. All we ask for is dry socks and a place to sleep. Don't Let the war news excite you we are going to wrap this thing up soon. We are too good for the Huns.

Love Freddy

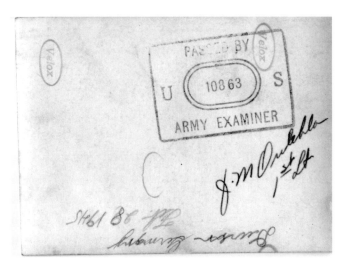

Both Roland and Frederick had to contend with Army censorship. The handbook Army Life *explains, "As time goes on, you will learn many details of our military activities—trivial things in themselves, but things which would add up to a complete story of our operations if they fell into the hands of spies or saboteurs" (p. 15). Another passage in the handbook instructs soldiers: "Don't Worry the Folks at Home" (p. 46). Thus Frederick was not permitted to disclose where he was in his letters, and when Roland occasionally developed a photo overseas to send to his mother, it had to be cleared by the Army's censors. Frederick's letter of December 24, with its poignant description of homesickness, was modified so as not to "worry the folks at home."*

December 23, 1944

Dear Marie,

I received the family letter saying that the family had made the sacrifice of eating Chicken instead of Turkey thanksgiving. What gave you the idea I had Thanksgiving Turkey. Today for the first time in a month I changed underwear. We were brought to a shower point Where we all took a bath. We turned in all our clothing and received a complete set of clothing, underwear to shirt. It feels good to have clean clothes on. Its just a little thing; but it means everything to us. No mail today; but when it comes It will come in a big bunch. Thats all for now.

Love Freddie

December 24, 1944
Somewhere in Germany

Dear Dot,

I might as well tell you now that I am in Germany. You probably have been worrying about me being in the battle for Belgium. Don't worry about me or those boys in Belgium, by the time you get this you will probably be reading about a smashing victory there instead of Defeat.

It's Christmas Eve & I'm spending it in a bombproof shelter. We have a radio and we heard Bing Crosby ~~tear the heard out of the boys with~~ sing. [edit by Army Examiner] White Christmas. It really is a heart breaker. The short waved Christmas carols. Really have the boys thinking of home. Its pretty Melancholy; but its necessary to make sure that next year the boys that have spent three Christmases here will be home for good. This will be the last one here. Next year we will be together.

Love Freddy.

~

December 25, 1944
Germany

Dear Ma, and Pa and Sisters,

Well this is the first Christmas That we have been separated. No doubt you are praying as I am that it will be the last one. We have been extremely blessed by God. We are all alive and well. We still love one another. When this war is over, we can easily pick up all the loose threads and weave a fiber that will make even stronger bonds to tie us together.

Today I am just one of the millions of boys who are doing their best to give us all a better world to live in. We are going to do IT.

I guess you are probably worried about the stories in the papers. There is no doubt that this is the most serious test that we have had to face. We are a confident and determined army. We can beat them. We are too good for anyone to beat us. The enemy is making his last desperate attempt. Way down deep in their heart, they know their days are numbered. It is just a matter of time before he stops his struggle. I spent Christmas quite peacefully. I didn't have a chance to go to church. I spent my

> No, it wasn't much of a Christmas, but, we still made the most of what we had. Headquarters wire crew kept it alive when Corso and Wolcott decorated a tree. It wasn't much of a tree and the decorations weren't so hot, but, it sure was a darned beautiful thing to see.
>
> —*The 309th Field Artillery Battalion*, p. 36

Roland often had pictures taken of himself, with or without a friend. He would have these photos developed and send them home to assure his family that he was well. Here he poses on a captured German howitzer with a friend.

During the intense fighting of the Battle of the Bulge, radio operators such as Frederick directed artillery fire from an elevated position in town. In Lammersdorf, Germany, battalion operations were directed from this church steeple. Photo from The 309th Field Artillery Battalion, *p. 40.*

meditation on the rosary and the bible. I spent the morning listening to the Christmas Carols over the radio. We had a beautiful dinner turkey all the fixings. Nuts and cake. The cooks really took care of us.

It was an unusual Christmas. It really is an experience that I wouldn't miss for the world. I am only a small cog around here, the other cogs have been grinding longer than I have. Some of the boys have been overseas three Christmases. That stage is past. So all in all we should thank God for our lucky lives. Pray that he keeps on delivering his blessings on us.

Love Freddy.

~

Somewhere in Germany
Dec 29, 1944

Dear Dot,

The weather continues to be perfect for us. We have been having clear cold weather. The airforce is out in great force. I received Edna's U.S.O. letter and your letter of the 20th. Forget about your fears of the German breakthrough. I'm not in its path. I wouldn't worry about it. Me thinks that this temporary victory of the Germans Is going to be turned into one of our greatest victorys. The radio programs have been improving. We even heard the Hit Parade.

Love Freddie

~

Somewhere in Germany
Jan 3, 1944 [sic].

Dear Marie.

I went to visit an outfit near here that had a bunch of boys from Lawrence and East Adams, Mass. We had a nice time talking about the home towns. When they found out I just left the states in October they piled me with questions. They asked about woman strikes, steaks. They were really hungry for the latest news. They had no idea how things were. They got a great big kick out of the predictions of the people in the states about the war. They were mad about V E day.

Love Freddy

~

Jan 9, 1945

Dear Dot

Received a U of Conn. paper and Edna's letter of Dec 22.

I have read in the papers of the Cold and snow back home. We can match it; but were dressed for it. Winter is hard on the civilians in Europe. I guess I'll never be a good soldier. I don't know to hate. I feel depressed when I see churches flattened down and homes wrecked and burned. Old people and young people carrying their possessions on their back or pulling it on sleds behind them; but these were the same people who cheered the wrecking of Warsaw, the burning of London. I guess I'll learn to hate.

Love Freddy

~

Somewhere in Germany
Jan 23, 1944 [sic]

Dear Dot,

I'm doing fine. I didn't receive any mail today. The boys are all inthused about the Russian victories. We feel that they will help shorten the war greatly. I read in today's paper where the people in the states feel that the war isn't going to last long again. Good

The winter of 1944–45 was one of the worst on record, which created hardships for the troops. There were many weather-related injuries among the Americans. Above, a member of the 348th bundled up outside headquarters in Banneux, Belgium. Below, Roland's friends try to keep warm around a makeshift stove outside Düren. It is characteristic of Frederick that he thinks of other people's discomfort rather than his own.

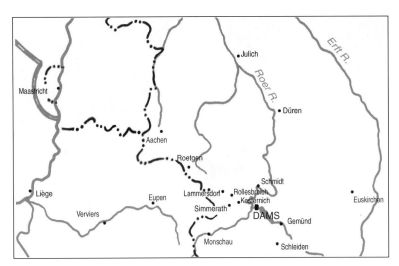

Somewhere in Germany: While Roland and the engineers stayed in the Liège area to clean up the destruction, Frederick moved west with the artillery toward the dams on the Roer River

old civilians. They can't make up their mind about the war. They work, then slack, then work then slack off. It would be much better for the war effort if we didn't publish our victories: so they would settle down and work at a steady rate. Thats all for now.

Love Freddie

P.S. Send me snapshots of you and the family.

~

Somewhere in Germany
Jan 28, 1945

Dear Ma,

Everything is fine and Dandy. I didn't receive any mail today; but very few of us receive any. I went to church this morning and received communion. Services were impressive.

Its impolite to write in pencil; but I haven't any ink. Send me a bottle of ink; and a fountain pen.

I am running out of words. I just like to say is pray hard, your as near to God as any person is.

Love Freddy

~

Somewhere in Germany
Jan 31, 1945

Dear Pa,

Everything is still going along fine. You probably know what's doing in Europe by Reading the papers. You see an overall picture of the war. We only see a limited sector. I have made bets this war would be over by March twentieth. I haven't lost a bet in Europe yet.

Received no letters; but received two papers. One was from the Navy Yard.
Try writing V mail.

Love Freddie

Somewhere in Germany
Feb 2, 1945

Dear Dot,

I have a lot of news tonight to spill. It will answer a lot of your questions. I am
now in the ninth (9th) Army. I cant tell you specifically where I am; but the enclosed clippings with the aid of a map of Germany will give you a good location.

We have fought the Germans in the Siegfried Line and beaten them. We
have ripped out a great big chunk of the defenses before Berlin. We have captured
over 500 hundred "Nazi Supermen?" They look pretty poor to me. If all the Divs.
do as good as we do, I think we can wind this war over soon. We all face the future
with confidence. We have the feeling we are the best division in the best army.

I didn't receive any letters today; but I received the Boston Globe and a nice
package from Ma's lodge.

Enclosed are some S & S clippings and souvenirs.

Love Freddy

Somewhere in Germany,
Feb 15, 1945

Dear Pa,

I'm still fine and dandy. The weather gives a promise of an early Spring.
There was very little mail today. I didn't receive any: so I read yesterdays mail

*A German sniper captured by a 348th combat engineer in Belgium in
February 1945. Roland's picture and Frederick's letter give a clear in-
dication of the state the Germans had been reduced to by this time, both
mentally and physically.*

Valentine's Day, 1945. This sketch of army life was included in a Valentine letter sent home to Frederick's mother in February 1945. Throughout his life, Frederick displayed no such artistic skills. We assume that another GI sketched the picture while Frederick signed the letter. Frederick, who was verbally quite gifted, would often write letters for the other soldiers to their wives, families, and girlfriends back on the homefront—another example of how our GIs helped one another out.

again. I read the Navy Yard News. It made me mad. All they talk about is the Jap War. Don't they know the European war is still on. Another thing that got me mad was that the Yard couldn't get enough workers. There's enough people working in Night clubs, Bowling alley's and movies to get thousands of war workers. The Boston Globe didn't do me any good. All the pictures showed the soldiers being kissed by the French women, riding bikes with Dutch Girls. They are the lucky soldiers on pass. Why don't they show the boys doing their regular duties.

Love Freddie

~

Somewhere in Germany
Feb 18, 1945

Dear Dot,

Things are still going fine. I received one early January letter. Yesterday I received a large amount of mail. I received Edna's valentine and a couple of letters with Life Magazines pictures of the Army Navy Football games. Some sneaky, low down, snoop saw the bulkiness of the valentines and the clippings and thought there might be money or valuables in it. I hope next time the lousy crook slits open letters, to see if there are any valuables in it, he breaks his wrist reaching for the letter. I know for sure that the dirty work wasn't done by anyone in this battalion. I know the mailman personally. He is honest. Its the U.S. end of it I do not trust.

Love Freddy

~

Somewhere in Germany
Feb 27, 1945

Dear Ma,

I'm still doing fine and dandy. I received a nice bunch of mail. I received six letters today. I received Maries letter of Feb first, and Dots letter of Feb twelfth. I also received Evelyn Mulveys letter from February eighteenth and a couple of the small Boston newspapers from Gerry and Margret Mc Caffrey. Now that Spring is coming I think it would be best to send my mail air mail. If you don't send them V mail; but never send them by regular mail. It takes months.

I was listening to the radio today when I heard a record played called "Angelina." Half of it was in Italian and the rest of it was in American swing. It was a beautiful record. What else could it be when it is connected with the name of Angelina. The record only lasted three minutes but I kept on dreaming for a half hour about you. To tell you the truth I'm really not in this war. My body is here; but my mind is thousands of miles away with you, pa, and the kids.

I change European time into American time and imagine I'm home with you. When I go to bed at eleven, Its six o'clock in Boston. I just imagine I'm in the kitchen watching you. I sit down at supper and eat with you. I'm never lonely. Each night I know I am one day nearer home. It won't be long now. All the armies are moving. We will get it over soon.

Love Freddie

P.S. I'm now using your stationery.

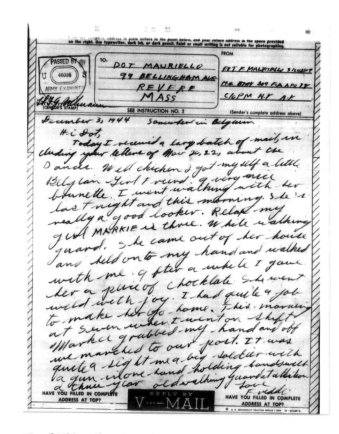

V mail: This mail service used during the war to and from U.S. Armed Forces overseas reproduced letters on microfilm. The letters were then enlarged on photographic paper for delivery. This service allowed the boys overseas to keep in touch with their families relatively quickly—of great importance for homesick troops and worried families.

Chapter Four

To Berlin!
The River Wars

(March 1945–April 1945)

URING MARCH AND APRIL 1945 the Allies raced towards Berlin as Hitler's once-great armies surrendered by the millions. However, the final defeat of Germany necessitated the crossing of a series of heavily defended rivers, most notably the Ruhr and Rhine Rivers, running through the heart of Germany's industrial valleys. On the other side of the rivers lay a devastated Germany—surrendering German soldiers; Jews and other victims of Nazi genocide; emaciated Russian and East European slave laborers; and homeless civilians and children. Once-beautiful cities were reduced to rubble. The photographs and letters in this chapter document the human and material costs of the most destructive war in history.

The period from March 1945 through the end of April 1945 was one of the busiest and most dangerous for the 348th Engineering Combat Battalion. Again, the photographs reveal what Roland found significant and meaningful to his war experience. They document the battalion's instrumental role in building temporary bridges across the Ruhr, Sieg, and Rhine Rivers, allowing Allied forces to push into the heart of Germany. The photographs from this period reveal the precarious nature of these bridges and the often dangerous conditions under which they were built. In one revealing photograph Roland provides a soldier's eye-view across a pontoon bridge spanning the Ruhr River. From this photograph we get a sense of how dangerous it must have been to build and then cross this bridge under enemy fire. Roland also photographs a member of the 348th on a bulldozer and crews repairing damaged roads as the U.S. Army moved east.

The photographs in this chapter also document the tragedy of war and Roland's perception of the human and material costs of war. He takes a number of interesting photographs of abandoned or captured German equipment and weapons. These photos represent two sides of the Allied victory: pride in defeating the German enemy, but also an awesome sense of having fought and beaten one of the world's most sophisticated and dangerous war machines. The photograph of a com-

Company A was under sniper and artillery fire as it entered Rolsdorf, a suburb of Düren, on March 1. Roland saw sporadic action as a rifleman for the 348th Combat Engineering Battalion.

The photograph on the previous page shows a timber bridge built by Company A across the Ruhr River between March 2 and March 8, 1945.

rade standing next to an enormous captured artillery shell reveals at once the awesome power of the new technology of war and the human courage to defeat it.

Another set of photographs documents the human side of an occupying army. Roland goes out of his way to photograph groups of young children either orphaned or displaced by war. Other photographs document the destruction of German cities and towns by Allied air and ground bombing. Roland's sense of history is also revealed in this part of the collection. He powerfully juxtaposes an untouched statue of a German national hero against the backdrop of the destroyed town of Düren.

There are also photographs that represent the important sense of comradeship among victorious soldiers. There are a number of shots of U.S. GIs smiling with the knowledge that the German enemy is retreating and that the war in the European Theater will soon be over. There are also photographs that document the historic meeting of the U.S. and Soviet armies at the Elbe River during the last days of April. Company A was responsible for ferrying the 82nd Airborne Division and units of the Red Army across the Elbe River. There is a rare photograph of members of Roland's battalion posing with victorious Red Army troops. There is no sense of the imminent Cold War between the United States and the Soviet Union that was to follow in the years after World War II. Instead, the photograph reveals only a sense of comradeship between soldiers who have fought for the same objective and won.

Frederick and the 309th Field Artillery Battalion were crossing the bridges that engineering units like Roland's were building. On March 21, 1944, the 309th crossed the Remagen Bridge over the Rhine River under heavy fire. Frederick's letters home three days later reveal the sense of confidence that GIs felt once they had crossed this last natural barrier before Germany. On the eastern side of Germany's rivers Frederick encountered the German civilian population. His letters reveal that he initially suspects that the civilians are all Nazi sympathizers and

The 348th entered Germany on March 1, 1945. Heavy shelling by both German and Allied artillery had caused a great deal of damage, and as the German Army retreated it destroyed roads and bridges to slow the Allied advance. Timely road and bridge repairs were critical for the Allies' successful push into Germany and ultimate victory.

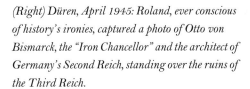

(Right) Düren, April 1945: Roland, ever conscious of history's ironies, captured a photo of Otto von Bismarck, the "Iron Chancellor" and the architect of Germany's Second Reich, standing over the ruins of the Third Reich.

(Above) 348th Combat Engineering Battalion Company A working on a bridge spanning the Sieg River outside Siegburg, March 1945.

(Below) Members of the 348th Combat Engineering Battalion at a U.S. Army depot in Siegburg, Germany.

lying about their involvement with Nazi ideology and support for Hitler. By May, as the war winds down, his letters home become more thoughtful and sympathetic to the civilians who had suffered over five years of war. The letters also reveal a humorous and playful side. In one April 17 letter home to his sister Dorothy, Frederick boasts, with a great deal of exaggeration, about his brave exploits in capturing German soldiers.

Some of the most compelling letters are from April 1945. Frederick's letters give voice to the scenes of defeated German soldiers surrendering the emaciated slave laborers and concentration camp victims, and, most of all, the shattered lives of civilians and innocent children. The tone of the letters becomes more serious and thoughtful as he reflects on the pervasiveness of Nazi ideology among the German people. For the first time he experiences war as a conqueror. Unlike Belgium in 1944, where they were received as liberators, he and other GIs were perceived by German civilians as the victorious enemy. In one April 22 letter Frederick, speaking of the German civilians he encounters, states "50% despise us and the other 50% fear us."

~

Somewhere in Germany
March 10, 1945

Dear Dot,

I'm still doing fine and dandy. Mail call really caught up with me last night. I received your letters of Feb 23 and 28th, letters from the fellows and a letter from Lt. Waldron. I have been receiving all the newspapers regularly.

I suppose you have been reading of our sensational work. We all are enthused. We are like a football team that has the ball on a touchdown drive. We took the ball on the one yard line and we carried it up to our fifty and now we are pounding deep into enemy territory. This is the touchdown drive and any day our next play will be the touch down play.

Well you really showed me up in song picking. I guess our music is old. The only fellow who heard "Accentuate the Positive" was one of the boys who heard Glenn Millers band in Paris. Have you heard two songs the army has "Chocklate Soldier from the U.S.A" and "When my Man Comes Home."

We have been living in the lap of luxury. We aren't sleeping outside we now have German homes to sleep in. We try to make it a practice of moving the civilians together and we live in separate homes. Sometimes we can not find room for the civilians and we graciously let them sleep in separate rooms.

We get along OK. These Germans were told they would be killed and mistreated by our troops. They do all they can to please us. This lady we live with brings up the coal, builds the fire, makes hot water and sweeps our floors every two hours. That is maid service that our best hotels don't give. I don't know if the civilians are scared of us and are trying to please us or they are really gratefull for being freed from the Nazis. I don't trust them. The army policy of firm friendly treatment with no fraternization is the best policy. No revenge purge but no kissing and making up. They started this thing. They have to pay.

Another interesting thing is to see all the different nationality soldiers who are around. They were rescued when we captured German prisoner camps. I met some Italian prisoners from Alvilino. They were telling us of the not so nice treatment from the Germans. They also told of great destruction of areas by our planes.

Thats all for now.

Love Freddy

Somewhere in Germany
March 11, 1945

Dear Marie,

I'm still doing fine and dandy. Things are still going beautifully. It gives us a great feeling to find out the army is doing so well.

A young boy on a bicycle crosses one of the many temporary bridges constructed by the 348th Engineers near Siegburg . . .

. . . and makes two new friends. The German children, initially afraid of the invading Americans, became much more open toward them. Especially in the case of the German children, most GIs eventually chose to ignore the official U.S. policy of nonfraternization.

The 348th stops to rest en route to the next bridge and road repair assignment in Germany.

We are still living in civilian homes that civilians have left. We don't mix in with the few civilians that are left. There aren't too many civilians. The Nazis take the civilians with them. The few that remain profess to be anti Nazis. We still don't trust them.

I just heard the news over the radio that after the European war men will be returned to the U.S for furloughs. Then be transhipped to the pacific. U.S here I come.

Love Freddie

~

Somewhere in Germany
March 13, 1945

Dear Marie,

I am doing all right and have everything under controll. I suppose you have been reading about the progress of the First Army. We are very proud of our record and intend to keep adding on to it.

The country side is different than that in which we have been. It is not the rugged hilly wooden sections, but rather plains and rolling hills. There are numerous Hamlets dotting the countryside. Now and then a large city. The German land along the Rhine is industrial. Across the Rhine River is the Ruhr Valley. The Ruhr Valley is to Germany as Pittsburg is to the U.S. When the armies capture it, The Germans should be pretty well out of the war. The Russians have the northern manufacturing districts and we will have the Southern districts. The German armies can not last long after that.

Most of the country people in Germany have been pretty lucky. They havent been bombed like the people in the large cities. Our air corp went after legitimate targets in the manufacturing cities and left these little Hamlets alone. This gives us a great chance to study German architecture.

The German homes compare favorably with ours. They usually are single family houses with seven or eight rooms. The kitchen is usually small and is downstairs with the Dining Room and sitting Room. Upstairs are all the bedrooms. Usually with each country house, there is a large attached barn. The barn has cows, horses, and chickens. The barn and houses are laid out in wings so that the final appearance is a quadrangle with a large court yard in the middle. The entrance to the court yard is accomplished by large swing doors. All in all its quite interesting; but I don't want one for me.

Love—Freddie

P.S. I just received Pa's letter of Feb 12th. Write V mail or air mail but never regular mail.

Roland and some other men in the 348th, by now fast friends, find time to simply enjoy each other's company.

Somewhere in Germany
With The First Army Chasing the German Army,
March 24, 1945

Dear Marie,

I received your regular mail letter of Feb. 21 and March 10th V mail. You see how much faster V mail letters and airmail letters are. Write airmail or V mail.

Today we are excited by more good news that really has us bursting with excitement. It seems everybody and his uncle have now crossed the Rhine. We are all enthused. The last big obstacle is gone. We are on our way.

The weather continues to be like May instead of March. The trees are starting to bud, and the few German civilians that are left are starting to plough the fields. Spring Feaver has me. The funny part of it is that I have time to sleep and take naps. War is much easier than I dreamed. Everyone knows their job perfectly. We do our tours of duty with smooth precision that gives us the maximum time for ourselves.

I have received more cigarettes and soap from our rations than I will ever

BRUNSWICK

(Top left) Roland brought home a set of postcards from Braunschweig (Brunswick), where he was stationed in April. The city had a number of important industries, and Allied bombing raids killed almost 3,000 inhabitants, and 90 percent of the city center was destroyed.

(Bottom left) The 348th camped outside Braunschweig in early April 1945.

(Above) 348th Combat Engineering Battalion with German children near Braunschweig in mid-April 1945.

Roland ferrying Allied troops and equipment across the Elbe River in late April or early May 1945. The Elbe was the last major barrier the Allies faced before Berlin.

use. It was a good thing we turned in our overcoats. I havent room in my bag anymore.

I'll close now.

Love Freddy

~

Somewhere in Germany—With the First Army
April 9, 1945

Dear Dot,

I'm still fine and dandy. I was very happy to receive your very recent letters of April first and April third. You must have smiled very prettily at the Post Office because six days from Boston to deep in the heart of Germany is record time. Don't flatter me so much in your letters. You will make me apply for the morale division.

Flowers were a small token for all the thoughtful deeds and acts you have done for me.

I should sue you for infringing my copywright laws. I thought you knew I have had offers for my clippings. I'm glad your friends and teacher enjoyed them. As much as your friends enjoy those tales, that is how much I am enjoying life. Maybe I should stop enjoying life and begin getting worried for four dollars and forty cents more a month. Tell your girl friend to keep that Junior prom date open. Now I have special inspiration to finish this war in a hurry. Imagine a buck private going to a Junior prom at Salem. That is equivalent to the congressional medal of honor. Now that I have been formally asked for a prom for the first time in my life, I'll be at the Longwood Towers for the Prom. If I cant make the Junior prom I'll make the senior reception next year. If you see Chubby give him my regards. Exactly what cute stories has his sister told you. There must be thousands of stories. What ones are they. I don't doubt they are very favorable.

German children were a constant photo opportunity for the 348th in late April 1945. These kids were hungry, and many of them were orphaned.

Well The lights are out and a candle might have been an inspiration to Lincoln but its merely an eye strain to me.

Love & Kisses

Freddy

~

Somewhere in Germany
April 12, 1945

Dear Dot,

I'm still in the pink. There is no mail tonight due to some red tape technicality. We will wait: tomorrow and get twice as much.

The war's pace is becoming faster. Today we have seen large columns of trucks loaded with prisoners going back. It was a most encouraging sign. They were definitely a sad looking beaten bunch. The roads are lined with slave laborers from Russia, Poland and other conquered countries on their way back to freedom. Hitler used millions of these impressed people to work his farms and factories. From their stories the Germans were mean monsters. They were beaten often. Long hours and short rations of food seem to be the general rule.

Love Freddy

~

Roland standing on a captured German railroad cannon in late April 1945.

Somewhere in Germany
April 13, 1945

Dear Marie,

The war is going along in grand style. We are all enthused about it. We have seen a lot of German prisoners going back. They knew the war was lost. All over the ground are signs of the German retreat. Gas masks, bullets, wrecked vehickles and smashed German rifles litter the ground.

The roads are lined with strings of slave laborers. The majority of them are Russian. Even the German Civilians know its the end and are getting on the American bandwagon. They are not causing Trouble. They all deny they're Nazis and want to be forgiven. I hope the people back home don't fall for that sympathy angle. We won't. We heard about the death of Roosevelt. We all felt it keenly. Its causing some discussion.

Love Freddy

Somewhere in Germany
April 16, 1945

Dear Ma & Pa,

I'm fine and dandy. I guess you know all about the war. Its really going as good as the papers say it is. All day long truck load after truck load of German prisoners pass by. I have seen prisoners cages that must have had thousands of them. They are a ragged and beaten lot.

Tonight I am in a beautiful German home. Its quite elaborate. Beautiful dining room tables, nice rugs on the floor and elaborate lamps. As usual there are the elaborate wood cabinets. That I have never seen the equal to in the states.

This is a very beautiful part of the country. There are lawn and flower beds; but in the center of towns, where the factory district was, its all ruins. The air corp really wiped out the factories. It was a neat job. The factories were all smashed; but the homes weren't touched.

The people here have really changed parties overnight. They all love the country of the United States and all hate Hitler. To listen to them talk you would think that there were no Nazi's in Germany. When you search their house for prisoners or guns they oblige with big smiles and help you immediately. The pay off was today we were standing talking to a young German girl about 9 or ten

These German soldiers were reduced to horse-drawn wagons when Roland documented their surrender in mid-April 1945.

years old who spoke English. Up comes a lady who talks to the girl in German and the Girl translates it to us. The lady wanted us to go over her house and sleep—she had three beds. A bed apiece. We turned that offer down cold. First place its forbidden to Fratanize and second it doesn't it appeal to me to fall asleep at the tender mercy of a German family. All the Germans want us to show Mercy. Its too late they should have thought it all over ten years ago.

Love Freddy

~

Somewhere in Germany
With The First Army chasing the German Army
April 17, 1945

Dear Eddie and Dot,

I'm a hero (?). I have captured three prisoners (fanfare of trumpets Ta Ta Ta). It wasn't much. Modesty permits me to say only it was the greatest piece, the most skillfully conducted, brilliantly planned maneuver in the whole history of the U.S Army. I am the apple of the staff's eye (if not the worm in the apple).

We came upon the three prisoners eating in a house of one of the prisoners girl friends (a nice dish she was.) Thats the advantage of fighting in your own country. When things get tough and the battle seems lost you always can run to your girl friends house. Her mother will keep strange men away from her daughter. Catching prisoners was nothing. Getting the guy away from his girl was the battle. She was crying and hanging on to him and kissing. I felt like a heel. Then with my Edward G. Robinson snarl and talking out of the corner of my mouth like I have been capturing prisoner's every day for ten years I told them to break it up. (Little did they know I have been practicing that Robinson snarl in front of the mirrors for weeks.) (Simply a killer. Congressional medal of honor material.) I let the prisoners out first and turned my back to them so I could watch the girl.

As Roland and his company pushed further west, German soldiers surrendered to the Allies. Here a captured German soldier sits atop a truck, guarded by a member of the 348th.

Knowing the way the man power shortage is, I figured that a girl who was lucky enough to have a man and then seeing someone taking away this rare creature, called boyfriend, is likely to get mad at the person taking him away and might do something desperate to keep him. I figured the least she would do is to crash a vase around my head. Believe me I dont mind having a vase bent around my ears. It would look much better than this inverted wash basin the Army calls helmets; but I figured that if the M.Ps caught me with a vase on my head. They would arrest me for wearing improper equipment (no sense of humor in the M.P corp).

Then came the triumphal march down the main street of the town. Down the streets passing between canyons of German homes with hundreds of pretty girls looking, clasping their hands and saying "my hero." (meaning the guys in front of me). I was a sensation. I wanted to bow and clasp my hands over my head like all the movie heroes do, but I needed two hands to hold my gun.

Then we came to a corner. My prisoners went around it first. They almost stepped on top of a G.I who was changing a flat tire. He looked up and saw three German soldiers. He gulped and dived for his gun. I jumped out and yelled "Don't shoot, you peasant. They are prisoners." He looked up and said "Thats a heck of a way to bring them in." Then I coldly looked at him and said "How do you know anything about the procedure of taking prisoners. Have you taken any." "No," He says. "Well Im an old hand at this" I reply and walk away. I left him deeply impressed.

Then there was the haughty air and triumphal flourish as I turned in my prisoners at head quarters. All the boys asked me for the story. In all modesty I told them the story in a few terse words, a terse ten thousand words.

Oh yes my reward. An hour later I received a nice bawling out for wearing one of the prisoners pistol. Thats gratitude for you. Biting the hand that feeds them. I have a good mind to quit and bring my talent to the Navy.

Love Freddy

~

A 348th Combat Engineer from Company A standing next to a railroad cannon shell, late April 1945.

Roland and his friends proudly display captured German Lugars. As is evident from Frederick's letter of April 17 and from many of Roland's photographs, captured German arms held an irresistible attraction for the young men.

Somewhere in Germany
April 22, 1945

Dear Marie,

I'm doing fine and dandy. No mail from home. I did get a few from Helen Walsh and the boys. Rita Waldron met Joe Waldron in Paris. It must have been quite a reunion.

The people in this time are unfriendly. 50% despise us, the other 50% fear us. When we walk down the streets little children of two and three go running into their house. I bet their mothers must have told them hundreds of boogey man stories. The American soldiers must have been the bogey man. I guess after a while they will find out that we aren't as bad as the Nazi's say. We still won't fratanize with them though. It was a rainy squally Sunday today. We did not have church today.

Love Freddie

Somewhere in Germany
April 22, 1945

Dear Pa,

I'm still fine and dandy. I received your letter of April 15 and Kathleen Mulveys letter of the eighteenth. That's some improvement in the service. If I can get packages all will be swell.

We boys over here all feel keenly the death of Ernie Pyle. He was the only reporter that wrote the war from an enlisted man's point of view. He was a great writer. No other reporter will ever take his place. He didn't take the glory of war for his subject. He personalized the army. His books are war classics. When he died the link between the soldier's feeling and civilian literature was broken.

We have German marks for money. They aren't doing us any good. We cant fratanize with the Germans to spend our money. Second place there is nothing here to buy. Money, any kind, is no damn good.

Thats all for now.

Luck & Prayers

Freddy

~

Somewhere in Germany
April 28, 1945

Dear Pa,

I'm fine and dandy. The radio continues to blast out good news. The Russian American link up. The unconfirmed report of the German's offer to surrender. It can't last much longer. We all feel that its worth fighting a little longer to make sure we get unconditional surrender.

No mail tonight from the family. Just a few newspapers.

Tonight I'm mailing home a report on the outfit. Where we have been and what we have done. It should answer many of your questions. We are quite proud of the record. It gave me a funny feeling to read all about the battles we were in, in the headlines of the Boston Globe. I couldn't tell you it was. The Sunday Globe had a 3 page story about us. The Feb. Sun headline read "Yanks Take Roer Dam" Remember that One. Then there were the headlines about the Inf. crossing the Rhine and the Remagen bridge heads. That was us.

Love Freddy

German marks: Roland brought home some German currency as a souvenir. The middle bill, a whopping 500,000 marks, is evidence of the inflation Germany suffered under. And as Frederick remarked, there was nothing to buy. He comments again on the scarcity of goods in his letter of June 12, 1945.

The 348th Combat Engineers, Company A, meets Russian troops and the 82nd Airborne Division on the banks of the Elbe River in Germany on April 30, 1945. As Frederick indicates in his letter of June 4, 1945, the Germans were afraid of the Russians, who were known for atrocities commited toward German prisoners of war. At this time, there was no suspicion of cold war between the fighting men of the Allies.

Chapter Five

The Collapse of the Third Reich

(May 1945–December 1945)

For both Roland and Frederick the last month of the war and the occupation of Germany that followed was a period of reflection. Roland had been overseas since November 1943 and Frederick since October 1944. During that time each had seen intense combat, friends killed, innocent civilians murdered and displaced, and the destruction of a once-powerful army and nation. The photographs and letters from this period reflect this sobering experience. They emphasize friendship among brothers in arms, sympathy for the plight of civilians caught in war, and recognition of the historic importance of their mission.

Roland's photographs from this period are intense and provide original insight into what ordinary soldiers saw and experienced in the final days of World War II. Sometime between May 3 and May 5 Roland entered and photographed the horrible scenes of the recently liberated Wöbbelin concentration camp outside Ludwigslust. While many soldiers from the 82nd Airborne and other units entering the camp wrote about their experiences then or later, Roland photographed what he witnessed. Piles of bodies and mass graves were the remnants of Nazi racial policy and racial warfare. Fortunately, we now have rare photographic evidence of this less well known camp within the Holocaust that killed millions of Jews and other innocent victims.

The chapter also includes compelling photographs of the destruction caused by the war. Cities and towns stood in absolute ruin from Allied bombing and house-to-house fighting. The collection also includes some candid photographs of Roland and the men of the 348th Combat Engineering Battalion. The faces in the photographs reveal a more experienced group of men than the ones who clowned for the camera at Camp Menselton in Swansea, Wales, in 1943. They had fought a war and they look it.

Frederick's letters from this period are intense and also provide unique insights into the experiences of an ordinary soldier. In probably the most revealing and emotional letter in the collection, Frederick reflects on the meaning and memory of the war on V-E Day, May 8, 1945. In this letter to his mother, he wants to make sure that the sacrifices made by soldiers are not lost amidst civilian celebration. In

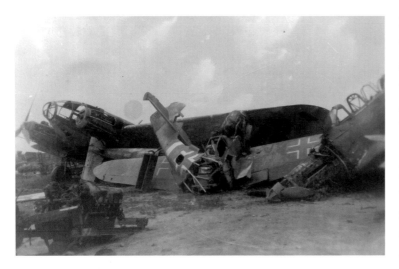

Roland's photo here captures wreckage at Waggum Air Base (a former Luftwaffe air base) outside of Braunschweig, where the 348th was stationed in mid-May 1945. The Germans destroyed as much as they could during their retreat to keep it out of enemy hands as part of the continued scorched-earth policy employed by the German Army since late 1943.

his words, "Today should be a day of prayer instead of revelry. Prayers to God. Prayers of Thanksgiving. Thank God that so many of us have been spared. Thank God the war never touched our homeland. Prayers for those who gave all to their country. Those whose ears and eyes have been closed by the touch of death. May God have mercy on their souls. Remember them in your wild reveling."

The letters that follow are from the occupation of Germany, which Frederick participated in from May 1945 to December 1945. They reveal the combination of relief, boredom, and resentment that many GIs felt being compelled to stay overseas after the war. Writing from Kassel, Germany, where he spent most of the postwar period, he vents his frustration at watching German soldiers return to normal civilian life and their families before he can. He rails against the U.S. policy of non-fraternization as shortsighted and bound to create resentment among servicemen and civilians. He consciously breaks the policy and forges friendships with a German family, especially the children, who must remind him of his own sisters.

Some of the later letters include photographs of Frederick and his buddies in the 309th Field Artillery Battalion. They show a playful side of the occupation force: Frederick in his now famous top-hat and red goatee, pictures of each other in captured German army uniforms holding Nazi banners, and daily life in Kassel and Niederelsungen.

Both Roland's photographs and Frederick's letters and accompanying photographs from this era share a common theme. The war was won and experienced by ordinary men. They fought, played, cried, and sometimes died among their battalions. They would never forget or let the world forget what they had experienced.

Somewhere in Germany
May

Dear Marie,

I'm still doing fine and dandy. I have just seen a city that was hit by one of our large air raids. You never in your wildest dreams imagined anything like this. It is utterly devastated except in the suburbs where there are three or four houses still standing in a small group. Large three and four story buildings are mere stone piles. Great blocks of houses are nothing more than a pile of rocks. Blocks of apartment houses seem to be untouched until you get close to them. Then its like a bit of stage scenery, there is no back or side just the front.

Love Freddy

Photograph of a destroyed German house sent home with Frederick's letter during the summer of 1945.

Victory Day
May 8, 1945

Dear Ma,

Today the war in Europe is over! All over the world people are celebrating. There are bands, speeches and parties. The civilian population has gone mad with the spirit of victory. Everyone is yelling "We won the war."

Everyone is enthused except we who did the fighting. The boys are quiet and subdued. No speeches, no wild shouts or wild singing. Its quiet. We have waited too long for victory to come. The battle for victory was fought weeks ago. Peace is merely an after climax.

I don't know why; but the boys are not cheering. Instead of a Roman Holiday we have a work day. We are disappointed in ourselves. The way we feel about the ending of the war is one of the biggest disappointments in our life. We can't generate a feeling of excitement or enthusiasm. We seem tired and lazy. There seems to be no thrills left in life. Life seems to be a repetition of monotonous days. We have finished a gigantic task. The world's biggest bloodiest war. "Little man, what now?"

A war-scarred building in Braunschweig, Germany.

Friendships forged through fire: Roland and friends from the 348th, Frederick and friends from the 309th. They were strangers in 1943, bonded through their collective experiences of war and now of occupation.

The world pauses and takes a holiday. Not so the army. We are merely workmen who have finished their day's labor. A dull feeling of satisfaction for what achievements we have accomplished during our day of labor. We finished for the day; but tomorrow is another day and there still lies another gigantic task before us. We are merely pausing to gather strength for the tomorrow.

Today should be a day of prayer instead of revelry. Prayers to God. Prayers of Thanksgiving. Thank God that so many of us have been spared. Thank God the war never touched our homeland. Prayers for those who gave all to their country. Those whose ears and eyes have been closed by the touch of death. May God have mercy on their souls. Remember them in your wild reveling.

The war has cost an unimaginable amount of money. More than that it has cost lives and years of youth that can never be replaced. As I write my mind is bringing me back to my high school days. The days when the big struggle was football. The boys of that team that we called our own, are walking across the page. I can't see them; my eyes are blurred with tears. The boys of that team will never gather together as a unit to talk over past glories. They played the game too hard in the fields of Belgium and France. We miss them. They will only run and play in past memories. The game is over for them. They didn't even see the last touchdown drive. No, merely put their names in gold in the towns and cities' memorials.

Go on and celebrate. Tonight I live in recollections and memories. Tomorrow we continue to train for the task lying before us.

Love, Freddy

Somewhere in Germany
May 16, 1945

Dear Dot,

I'am still doing fine and dandy. Today I received your letter of May seventh. So you think the Navy Yard is grand. It doesn't appeal to me. I received two pack-

In early May, the 348th Combat Engineers with the 82nd Airborne Division entered Wöbbelin concentration camp outside Ludwigslust. There they witnessed first hand the horrors of the Nazi regime and its crimes against humanity. Roland's photographs bear witness to man's inhumanity to man and provide a visual record of these atrocities.

The Wöbbelin concentration camp, located about twenty miles east of the Elbe River, was only established toward the end of 1944, as an extension of the Hamburg-Neuengamme camp. It held more than 5,000 prisoners; for 1,000 of them, the liberation on May 2 came too late.

It is a somber group of young men in this photograph of some of the men of the 348th Combat Engineer Battalion, Company A, taken during the last days of the war.

ages today. One package was numbered 5. The other package was the package that contained the Jar of Ravioli. I havent opened it yet. I will try it tonight.

Censorship regulations have eased a bit. So I can tell you a bit about my past travels. Then I have nothing more to say.

Right now I am in <u>KASSEL</u> Germany. It is a large city. As large as LYNN & DORCHESTER ADDED TOGETHER. At one time It must have been a beautiful City. Now its a desolate, barren wrecked city. I don't think there are four dozen homes that are not damaged. You can stand on a hill and look for miles and see nothing; but wrecked homes and piles of rock that were homes. You can't imagine it. Try to think of down town Boston wrecked with only a few houses left standing in Chelsea. Thats the nearest picture you can imagine. I visited a hospital that was five stories underground by the ST Vincent De Paul Society. I wrote Marie a letter all about it. She will read it to you. Thats Germany. Wrecked above Ground she is going under ground.

I don't feel sorry for them. This is their dues coming to them from London and Coventry.

Right now I have a dream job. I'm guarding a brewery. (a place where they make beer). These former Nazi's have tripped all over them selves to serve us. When ever we are thirsty they offer us beer. They sweep our floors when it gets dirty. The part that amused me was that

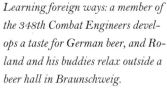

Learning foreign ways: a member of the 348th Combat Engineers develops a taste for German beer, and Roland and his buddies relax outside a beer hall in Braunschweig.

the janitor sprinkled beer all over the floor so the dust wouldn't rise. That's my idea of heaven. Don't worry we don't drink all the beer we want. We have officers down here every few hours checking on the guard.

Well I'll close for now.

Love Freddy

~

Somewhere in Germany
May 25, 1945

Dear Dot,

Today I became slightly mad. First we capture the Germans, Then we put them in the hospital to recover from their wounds. And today we discharge them from the German Army, make them civilians and send them home. I had twelve prisoners from the hospital I'm guarding. I was told to turn them over to the M.Ps who were to discharge them. The M.Ps wouldn't take them. Nobody would take them off my hands until they had discharge papers. After walking with them for an hour I got mad. I set down at a typewriter and wrote them each out a discharge and said get the hell out of here. Don't come back until the next war.

Love Freddy

~

Kassel Germany
May 31, 45

Dear Edna,

Well here it is the last day of May and I have just finished guard duty wearing a jacket and sweater. The weather has been unseasonably cold. We still see released German soldiers coming back to town. Its a funny feeling when we look at

Enjoying a taste of home: Roland and a friend take a few minutes to enjoy a good American game of baseball.

Allied forces used the German Autobahn to their advantage to quickly move much needed men and equipment during the occupation.

The U.S. depot in Braunschweig where Roland was stationed.

Roland and Frederick were much struck by the widespread destruction they witnessed in German cities and towns. Such scenes as the ones in Roland's photographs were commonplace as the Allies moved through Germany. Much damage was due to Allied air strikes; further destruction was the result of house-to-house fighting as the Allies sought to clear up pockets of German resistance.

each other. It isn't hate. It isn't friendliness. You feel indifferent. I try to imagine their feeling if I were in their shoes. It seems to me they are tired; but they must have an embarrassed feeling when they look at the civilians. They promised them world domination instead they gave them wrecked cities and hungry people.

Love Freddy

~

Kassel Germany
June 4, 1945

Dear Dot,

I received your letter of May 28th. One week service is damn good. I guess you must smile at the mailmen and they give you that "just for you extra special service." So your going out with the aristocracy. Navel officers from M.I.T. I hope you speak to me a lowly P.F.C after this war. I consider that P.F.C rating so lowly that I don't even put it on my return address and refuse to sew that stripe on my shirt. What gets me mad is that I wasn't given a chance to refuse the promotion.

My Goatee is causing more than a flutter in this army; and also among the civilians. The civilians think I'm a Russian. When I go down the streets mothers gather up their young ones and go indoors. Tonight I was out walking in the woods when I passed two girls on a bench. They looked up and saw me; they yelled "Russky", screamed and ran.

Its causing consternation among the officers. They cant stand the sight of a red beard. Strange officers come up to me and want to know if I'm Russian or American. They give me all kinds of hints to take it off. They say it looks rotten and adjectives like that going down the line. I just smile and agree with them. The only way it comes off is with a direct order. They can't give that order; because some one 150 years ago made the order that American soldiers can have beards. Its going to take some time, trouble, and money to change the orders just for me.

Both Frederick and Roland experienced the ambivalence the Germans and the victorious Allies felt for each other. This feeling is evident in Roland's compelling photo of German townspeople in Regensburg, April 30, 1945.

Frederick sporting his famous red goatee. According to the 309th Field Artillery Battalion history, "Mauriello grew so fond of his bright red chest tickler that he will probably wear it until he gets home."

Three million soldiers in Europe and I'm the only one that has a beard. I intend on taking this home.

I guess you might think I'm conceited; because I send all these pictures home. I'm not. These are pictures taken of me by other boys. Do exactly as I tell you on all the pictures I send home. Some pictures I will send home will be prints and negatives. Some others will be negatives. The negatives I send home and say do not print. Put them in a separate envelope and mark them because I have already have sent the pictures. The negatives I send home mark print. Bring them to the store to have them developed and put those negatives in a separate envelope and mark those "Printed at Home." UNDERSTAND.

Two months ago I sent home some negatives of me and the boys in German uniform. One of those pictures is of RIVERA. Rivera is the spanish kid I took a picture with in full uniform and packs on our backs at Camp Pickett. Compare pictures of the German UNIFORMS with the one of Rivera and I decked out and you will recognize the picture. Send IT to me. Better still send me the pictures of us in German uniforms and I will give him his. Have you mailed those pictures of the Rhine River to Quist's and Power's house.

Write me about it

I received a letter from Mac Elwell today. He is fine. So isn't John Leonard. Thats all for now.

Love Freddy

P.S. Don't develop these negatives, you have them.

~

Kassel Germany
June 5, 1945

Dear Edna,

I'm slightly mad right now. After finishing my few hours of guard duty at the hospital, I laid down to get a few hours of sleep. I had just finished tossing around and became comfortable when the familiar cry rang out "Mauriello, come here. I have a job for you." I dressed up and went out to find out what this important job was that disturbed my sleep. There stood two German nurses who wanted to take a walk in the woods. Since they couldn't go out alone I had to go with them. So after walking 4 hours I walked some more. We walked five miles and picked flowers. How Sweet! Who won the war? An American girl can't get a soldier to take her walking every time she feels like it. But the German Girls can.

Love Freddy

Frederick hunting a less deadly enemy—dinner—after the war outside Kassel, Germany.

Kassel Germany
June 12, 1945

Dear Ma,

I'm still O.K. I received two of your packages today. I only ate a little of each one. I don't know the numbers yet. I will tell you them tomorrow. They had a lot of popcorn bars and dates. They are good; but the packages make good dessert. We don't need desserts we need food. Send me packages like you did at first. Pepperoni, Prowala or Velveta cheese. Stuffed or canned olives. Chocklate bars and stuff like that. Our food supply is cut 10%. The boys are all hungry. We all have hundreds of dollars in our pockets and cant buy a damn thing.

I'll write you a little bit about my German family. I'm father to about a dozen kids around here. When my truck pulls up to the station all the little girls and boys come running up crying Fredrick. They want me to give them piggy backs and play with them. I do. The German civilians think I'm crazy. They havent seen any soldier play with kids yet be he German or American. Everything is complete. My officers think I'm crazy and now the Germans do. And the people who don't think I'm either are mad at me for wearing a beard.

I have four little girls ranging from 6 to 10 years old that are my particular favorites who insist on sitting beside me where ever I go. A little red head six. Dorothy about eight. Einer and Hildergarde about ten. Hildergarde has beautiful

Frederick and a fellow soldier washing clothes with his "adopted" German family near Kassel.

blonde pig tails and a beautiful voice. She and Einer combine and sing to me in German. I have never heard such sweet music. Hilder is very poor. She lives in a small room in a barn with her mother and sick little brother. She has a heart of gold. Today when I gave out chocklate to the kids she didn't gulp it down like the rest of the kids. She ran into her house and gave it to her little sick brother. You will never know how much courage and unselfish intention that took. That was the first candy she had seen in years. Instead of enjoying herself and eating the candy that little girl put her own little brother's enjoyment before her own. She truly is a lady. I tell you Ma my eyes got a little wet to see something like that. We the smart grownups could take a lesson from these dumb kids. We have bombed their homes, killed their fathers and wrecked their lives and these kids think we're good.

My Government told me to hate these kids and not to speak to them. I'm not going to do it. They can court martial me and fine me; but I'll still be good to these kids. They should not be punished for the sins of their Parents. The American plan of Non Fratinization will prove to be one of our biggest mistakes. It can not be carried out. The American soldiers can not be cruel or brutal. In a short time you will see the rules changed.

The hope of the world and the dreams of peace lie with these children. We can educate them to see the true way of life or we can ignore them and lay the seeds of ignorance that will sprout and Flourish another war.

Love Freddy

Kassel Germany
June 14, 1945

Dear Ma,

I'm still O.K. Mail hasn't been too plentiful lately. The outfit hasn't received any mail for two days. We are plenty mad about it. During the war when we didn't get mail we believed them when they said they needed the trucks for carrying stuff to the front. Now there is no excuse for them not delivering mail to us. Mail is the only thing we care about. We work all day and the only thing that breaks up the monotony are the letters we receive at night.

I read in the papers about the U.S. is all excited about the policy of fratanization and American soldiers going out with German girls. Well I'll tell you. Our policy of non fratinization is all wrong. It is the worst policy we could have devised. It is hurting the American Army more than the German. If the government don't change the policy the soldiers will. The stories of American soldiers going out with German girls are greatly exaggerated. If you get caught talking to Germans you are fined a large amount of money. This is all wrong. For three or four years the boys have lived in deserts, mountains and fields that were full of blood and death. Dead and wounded Americans and burn't out cities were the only things they saw. We lived an animals existence.

Now the war is over. We are in cities where we have a chance to talk to other human beings beside soldiers. A chance to talk to mothers and fathers like you, a chance to hold little children in our laps. A chance to talk to a girl that resembles your sister or girl friend back home. A chance to become moral again. What happens? Some politician in Washington who has everything he wants. His family. Food, nightclubs, recreation says No! Generals in Paris and England who live in large cities and go out playing golf, dancing and talk to a friendly civil population say No! They say the Army will supply entertainment and recreation. What a Joke. Stories of us dancing and talking to American girls are nothing but lies. If by a miracle some Red Cross Girls do show up, they are taken over by the officers. They don't mix with the enlisted men. When there are Army Nurses in the neighborhood, it doesn't do us any good either. They are officers and we aren't supposed to have anything to do with them. Our officers entertain them with par-

SPECIAL ORDERS FOR GERMAN-AMERICAN RELATIONS

1.   To remember always that Germany, though conquered, is still a dangerous enemy nation.

a.   It is known that an underground organization for the continuation of the Nazi program for world domination is already in existence. This group will take advantage of every relaxation of vigilance on our part to carry on undercover war against us.

b.   The occupational forces are not on a good-will mission.

2.   Never to trust Germans, collectively or individually.

a.   For most of the past century, Germany has sought to attain world domination by conquest. This has been the third major attempt in the memory of men still living. To many Germans, this defeat will only be an interlude-a time to prepare for the next war.

b.   Except for such losses of life and property suffered by them, the Germans have no regrets for the havoc they have wrought in the world.

c.   The German has been taught that the national goal of domination must be attained regardless of the depths of treachery, murder and destruction necessary. He has been taught to sacrifice everything-ideals, honor, and even his wife and children for the State. Defeat will not erase that idea.

3.   To defeat German efforts to poison my thoughts or influence my attitude.

a.   The Nazis have found that the most powerful propaganda weapon is distortion of the truth. They have made skilful use of it and will re-double their efforts in the event of an occupation in order to influence the thinking of the occupational forces. There will probably be deliberate, studied and continuous efforts to influence our sympathies and to minimize the consequences of defeat

b.   You may expect all manner of approach—conversations to be overheard, underground publications to be found; there will be appeals to generosity and fair play; to pity for victims of devastation: to racial and cultural similarities; and to sympathy for an allegedly oppressed people.

c.   There will be attempts at sowing discord among Allied nations; at undermining Allied determination to enforce the surrender; at inducing a reduction in occupational forces; at lowering morale and efficiency of the occupying forces; at proving that Nazism was never wanted by the "gentle and cultured" German people.

4.   To avoid acts of violence, except when required by military necessity.

For you are an American soldier, not a Nazi.

5.   To conduct myself at all times so as to command the respect of the German people for myself, for the United States, and for the Allied Cause.

a.   The Germans hold all things military in deep respect. That respect must be maintained at all times or the Allied Cause is lost and the first steps are taken toward World War III. Each soldier must watch every action of himself and of his comrades. The German will be watching constantly, even though you may not see him. Let him see a good American Soldier.

American GIs were given specific instructions on how to treat the Germans. Many of them felt the policy was unjust and ignored it. Frederick, who came to oppose the idea of non-fraternization, received this statement of the U.S. policy as part of the occupational forces.

ties. The part that hurts is to make a good impression on the nurses they send details of men to work at the hospital. Nothing is too good for their girl friends as long as we do the work.

So all in all the policy of non-fratenization is no good and the only person it is hurting is the enlisted man of the US Army.

Thats all for now.

Love Freddy

P.S. The package you sent yesterday was number eight and the other package packed in an olive oil can had cheese tee bits, chocklate, and deviled ham. It didn't have a number.

Volkenburg Holland
June 30, 45

Hi Folks,

The Army has broken down and gave me a pass. I don't know how the Army will shift for itself while I'm gone. I have a three day pass here. Its a nice place for a rest; but its too quiet.

The trip was very interesting. We went through the Rhineland, Cologne, and over the Rhine again. I have seen the famed Cathedral of Cologne. It is too beautiful to describe. The postcards and booklet you will receive will show you what it really looks like. The Cathedral's spires can be seen for a long way. Their height is really shown by the contrast with the utterly flattened city of Cologne. It stands symbolically the house of God standing over the ruins of Man.

The spires are a lace work pattern made of concrete.

The city of Cologne had over a million people in it at one time, now there are a few thousand. I don't know where they live. There are no houses just cellars.

We have a nice hotel room here. The meals are G.I. but they are prepared by civilians and served on plates and white tablecloths. It makes the fried baloney

Frederick washing his clothes in his helmet.

taste better. Yesterday for the first time in four months we had ice cream, it tasted swell.

They have two large beer gardens with dance floors and orchestras. There is also a country club with a swimming pool and a small lake for canoes and boats.

They have mass here every morning at a dutch church. Today they had a high mass and procession for an old couple that were celebrating their 50th wedding anniversary.

I'll write more tonight.

Love Freddy

~

Germany

August 8, 1945

Dear Pa,

All of us here are pretty excited over the news of Russia declaring War on Japan. We feel that the war will be over with in six or seven months. I think this is an optimistic view. With all the Russian manpower available in the Pacific I doubt if they will ever send us there. The invention of the Atom Bomb is also causing quite a bit of talk today. None of us understand it. I wonder if they are going to use atomic power in postwar industry?

Love Freddy.

~

Niederelsungen

August 8, 45

Dear Edna,

I received two packages today from home, one package had cheese sticks, pepperoni, lots of gum, a can of ravioli, and lots of biscourti. The

Roland and a friend display portraits drawn of them during a USO visit.

boys here are crazy over biscourti. I'm going to open the other package tomorrow.

A lot of us were happy with the announcements that the advocates of place time conscription had given up hope to pass compulsory military training. Boy I am really glad to see that our Congress is waking up to the fact that the militaristic trend of our leaders was bringing us to a fascist form of government.

I have seen too many rotten deals pulled in this army to ever want my son to be part of it. The army is not a democratic institution. It teaches class distinctions. We are not allowed in the same bars, dances or night clubs with officers, we can not live in the same houses, they eat their meals separate from us and enlisted men have to be waiters for them. This undemocratic way of life is even breaking down to the enlisted men. In some outfits there are special clubs and eating places for seargents. An informal frank poll in the room tonight revealed that most of the boys did not swear, or drink before leaving home. Now the boys confess they swear all the time and get drunk every time they get a large quantity of liquor.

Slowly but surely the Army was moving into civilian life. If the trend continued like it has in the past five years, You would never recognize our own country. The army was made to fight and not to play politics. It has been playing politics.

To put it frankly the Army doesn't know how to handle its men. They don't know how to get along with the public. They have deliberately lied and lied to the people on practically everything. Their handling of American soldiers in prison is nothing short of cruelty.

They as far as we are concerned do not need a ten million man army. Three or four million would be enough. 6 million at the most. They aren't discharging the men fast enough. It seems they don't give a damn about discharging either. They want to keep a large Army so all the officers can keep their ranks and commands.

You must vote against military conscription. Its perfectly all right to have a large standing army by means of a National Guard or C.M.T.C. We can get in a large army by other means than conscription.

Members of the 348th, Company A stand at attention at Waggum Air base in May 1945.

Tomorrow I will try to describe the rotten system of giving out medals in the army. It is so rotten that medals just cause laughter when we see a man wearing one.

Thats all for now.

Love Freddi

~

Frederick posing in his trademark tophat, cigar, and cane near Kassel.

Niederelsungen Ger.
Aug 11, 1945

Dear Dot,

Everyone is pretty excited here about the Japs offering to surrender. We threw a premature wild party last night. As a result we have been punished by having to go to bed at 10:30 every night with no radio and lights for one week. When the official news comes we are going to throw a wild party that will wake the dead. We no doubt will be court-martialed and fined twenty dollars. It will be worth it. I think I will turn in my P.F.C stripe anyway. I have until Monday to sew it on my uniform. I hate the heck to sew on one rotten stripe after seeing the other guys sewing on three without going through 1/25 the danger I have.

I received another package today. It had Bicourti; Tuna, Dates, Ravioli, Potato Sticks. It had no pepperoni. All the boys almost cried. Pepperoni is the favorite food here. (No mail today.)

Now for music. I am going to say I told you so. First my letters of July 44 said "My dreamers are Getting Better all the time." If you read my letters of April 45 You will remember I said Robin Hood and Angelina. They were songs that were going to be hits.

If you remember two months ago I recommended "This Heart of Mine." I said It Again By Vaughn Monroe. Have you any new songs to beat those.

I'll close now.

Love Freddy.

Frederick and a fellow soldier of the 309th Field Artillery Battalion show off a captured Nazi flag.

Niederelsungen Germany
Aug 14, 45

Dear Pa,

We are still sitting around waiting for the Japanese war to end. Its really a sweating out Job. We have our ears glued to the radio. Its really more nerve wracking than the war. I was pretty well excited about a report over the radio last night stating that after the war the Point score would be dropped to <u>50</u> points. from the present 85. I have exactly 50. This is only rumor. There are still 700,000 85 point men who havent been shipped as yet. All we can do is sit and wait.

Tomorrow is a holiday here. Its the third anniversary of the forming of the division. We are having a half a day off in the morning and a picnic in the afternoon with races etc.

We had a parade today. It was a joke. They awarded bronze stars (medals) to the battalion. The boys laughed out loud when they saw who were getting them. There are about 3 officers to 100 men in a battery; but when the medals were given out 3 out of every 4 medals were given to officers. The boys were really disgusted. It was the rottenest piece of politics we have ever seen. As far as we were concerned the men that got them were cowards. Most all of them never went near the front. They merely put each other in for medals. I was a front line operator. I never seen them. In 140 days of Combat I seen these medal holders up front only one day and then the Germans were retreating.

The laughter and comments by the boys in the ranks during the ceremony was so loud that tonight our commander called a meeting of the seargents to bawl them out for allowing the men to talk during the presentation of medals. They never figure out maybe the boys talk because things are so rotten that the men have to say something.

Chances are I could have had a medal; but I talked myself out of it. Now when I see who have the medals I'm glad not to be in that group.

Thats all for now.

Love Freddy

~

Germany
Sept 10, 1945

Dear Marie,

I'm back at work at the newspaper. I received a package, today, number 15. Something has gone wrong with the last two packages. They havent been up to their usual standards. They have contained two one pound boxes of fancy cookies that take up half the packages. They had no pepperoni, olives etc. Its the Italian touch that we missed. This last package contained CIGARETTES. I DONT SMOKE.

The boys are hopping mad about the different Congressmen trying to change the point plan. Now its the boys 18 to 20 they want to let out. Last Night it was the married men. The night before it was all men over 26 to be discharged. The 20 to 25 group is really lost. Too old to go to school, too young to be married. All we did was fight the war.

Today we went to visit Prince Frederick's Palace twenty miles from here. It was really something. The lay-out plan was like the palace of Versailles.

The inside was truly amazing. The reception room was 100 ft long 50 ft wide. With cut glass chandeliers that sparkled with the reflection of the light. The walls had large oil paintings 25 ft by 25 ft long on the walls. They were even drawn on the ceilings. Along the other wall were hung tapestry 30 ft SQ showing Greecian scenes. There was another room. It was a gift of the Japanese government. It had all Japanese tables and furniture. At one end of the room was this throne setting. A huge Golden canopy supported by delicately carved wooden supports. Upstairs there was a Red Room, a blue Room and various different colored rooms with everything one color, these were bedrooms. The furnishings were worth hundreds of thousands of dollars. One table cost $40,000. It was made of Inlaid wood with exquisite designs of Mother of Pearl. All the rooms had oil paintings. One room had autographed pictures of all the royalty of Europe for the last 200 years. Its worth a fortune.

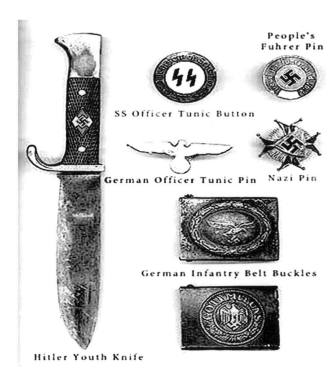

Roland's collection of Nazi memorabilia.

Frederick poses in a captured German uniform during the spring-summer of 1945.

The interesting part is that the two princesses who own it are Fanatic Nazis. They despise us. As punishment they, like all Germans in the village, have to go and clean the streets with a broom and shovel once a week. Its giving the Germans a real lesson in democracy.

Thats all for now.

Love Freddy

~

Niederelsungen Germ.
9/21/45

Dear Folks,

Hold on to your hats! I have some news. In five minutes last night the radio gave us more news than we have since we came over. First. The point score will be down to 60 points for discharge in November. The point system will be dropped this winter and men with over two years service will be discharged. Either way I cant lose, I will get out this winter. I have 58 points and will have 3 years Dec.

The army has said "men with 56 points will be taken out of all category I divisions (occupation) and transferred to another division that isn't occupation." That means I'll leave here soon to go to another division.

The army has announced that the 78 Division will go to BERLIN in OCTOBER. Thats one place I don't want to go to. Even our Major General dont want to go. There are Russian, English, French, American soldiers. The best divisions in the world are there showing off and trying to beat each other. They wear white shoe laces and white gloves. All that parade dress equipment. They want to give us 4 sets of uniforms. All we will do is stay in and wash equipment all day, parades, Marches, standing in streets at stiff attention in the snow and below zero weather. I'd rather fight another war than go through that.

When I wrote you for that money I didn't want you to go telling everyone about it. I merely told you to drop it in different envelopes. I knew you aren't supposed to do it. I wanted American in case I wanted to go on pass in these different countries. I could change it with other soldiers stationed there for that country's money. In case I got back to the states, I would have money on me. Instead of carrying large amounts of foreign money and waiting to have it changed. So drop me the money. I can use it.

Love Freddy

~

October 13, 1945
Giessen Germany

Dear Pa,

It is my first anniversary overseas. One year ago tonight I got a boat in New York to come overseas. I thought it would be a great adventure. I didn't think or imagine war and travel could be so boring. Everyday is the same here. Scenes and houses are alike all over the world. People are exactly alike except for languages. If I could get a crowd of Dutchmen, German, French and Englishmen together, make them keep their mouths shut, you couldn't pick out the different nationalities. But still these people in Europe have the crazy idea that they are better than the people of neighboring countries. Sometimes the borderline between two countries is only a street.

I had a day off during the week and took a trip with my time. I came across a small German city called Bad Hamburg. For the first time in my life I fell in love with a city. To me its the most beautiful city in the world. To the soldiers stationed there its nothing but an old overgrown town. I don't care what anyone calls it. Its still my favorite city. Its the only city I have seen in a year that hasn't any bombed houses, holes in the streets and wrecked skeleton walls to represent churches. Its a small clean thriving city of 20,000. It has homes, Parks, school neatly dressed children. No soldiers crowding the streets, and big army trucks to pour smoke out at you. It was civilization. By a freak of nature the war by passed it.

Roland's medals, from left to right, top to bottom: 150th and 348th Combat Battalion emblem; 348th Amphibious; 348th emblem; Time in Service; dog tag; Good Conduct & European Theater ribbons; combat engineer belt buckle; and Good Conduct medal.

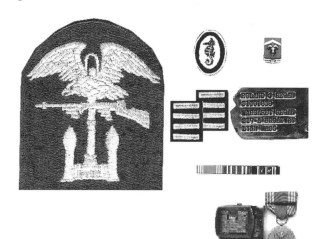

We ate in a transient mess. There were tables with table cloths, Waitresses to serve you and pour coffee from silver coffee pots into china cups. I havent been served like that since Holland. I was enjoying myself, then I became mad, and madder, why should a certain few have jobs like this, why should Military government units, Headquarters units, Special troops live like kings in towns like this, while the rest of us fought the war and when it was over instead of being rewarded with nice towns were forced to work in laundrys, warehouses, and storage depots. It isn't fair. Why should a few fight the war and carry the load alone, why cant we all carry the load.

The boys are pretty mad about the stevedores going on strike in N.Y. This is really causing havoc with the redeployment plans. There are thousands of soldiers tied up in the ports. The boys who were supposed to leave this month to go home from this unit have had their orders cancelled. The strike is pushing everyone back. This is a kick in the back to the army. Here we are forced to stay overseas while money hungry chiselers who have fat bank accounts try to squeeze out a little fatter pay check at our expense. Nice country we have.

So your going to be an usher with a tuxedo. You really are going to be a zoot suit kid and look real sharp. Ma better watch out or she will find you flirting with some chicken.

Thats all for now.

Love Freddy

~

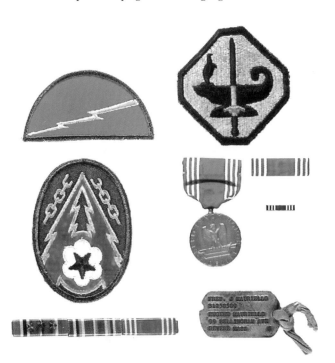

Frederick's medals and emblems, from left to right, top to bottom: 78th "Lightning" Division Patch; Specialized Training Program Patch; Communication Zone Europe Patch; Good Conduct Medal, Ribbon and Bar; European Campaign Ribbons; dog tag.

Giessen
Oct 20, 1945

Dear Folks,

Today is my 24th Birthday. My second one overseas. I know it will be my last one. It has been a most interesting year of life. I have travelled thousands of miles, been in six countries, seen all that was beautiful and all the rotteness of Human beings. Who knows, I might have seen the last war. I have seen the

On the way home: Happy members of the 348th bid Europe—and each other—fare-
well. Roland's company was among the first to be sent home because they had accu-
mulated more points than men who had arrived in Europe later. The photo at the
top right shows Roland in his backyard after his return home to Lynn.

Back to Boston: Frederick Mauriello on the way home (with Statue of Liberty in the background). The generation of Frederick and Roland was a unique one, shaped by their experiences in World War II.

shores of England and castles on the Rhine. I have seen a different season in different countries. I have seen different nationalities. The dignified Englishman, the passionate French, the excitable Belgians, the Hardworking scientific German. They all have something to teach; but none are models we should copy in entirety. The Shrewd mind of the German has its flaws. It has the military mind disease. Even today standing in the ruins of this city, a woman told me in 20 years Germany would have another army and another war. Thank heavens she is in the minority and holds an isolated opinion.

Another thing I learned is the small ordinary man is the same world over. He wants his home, family and security. He doesn't know how his own government is run; but he will fight to death for it.

All these atrocity stories can be told about all armies. In each army there are a certain group of cruel vicious men whose evil tendencies crop out when they are turned loose with a gun. They would be called killers and murderers but when they put on a uniform they are called soldiers and heroes.

Well thats all for one year.

Love Freddy

P.S. Today I received a letter from Pa, with 5 dollars in it. That makes $20. I also received a large pile of back mail also.

Select Bibliography

Primary Sources

Bryan, Keith. *Pack Up and Move: A Pictorial History of the 348th Engineer Combat Battalion.* Columbus, Nebr.: The Art Printery, n.d.

Frederick J. Mauriello, Sr. Collection of World War II Correspondence and Regalia, 1942–1945. John J. Burns Library of Rare Books and Special Collections, Boston College.

Roland J. Regan, Sr. Collection of World War II Photographs and Military Regalia. John J. Burns Library of Rare Books and Special Collections, Boston College.

Lightning: The Story of the 78th Infantry Division. Paris: Curian-Archereau, 1945.

309th Field Artillery Battalion: World War II European Theatre of Operations. Privately printed at the Rumford Press, 1947.

Secondary Sources

Abzug, Robert H. *Inside the Vicious Heart: Americans and the Liberation of Nazi Concentration Camps.* New York and London: Oxford University Press, 1985.

———. *America Views the Holocaust, 1933–1945: A Brief Documentary History.* Bedford Series in History and Society. New York: St Martin's Press, 1999.

Ambrose, Stephen. *Citizen Soldiers.* New York: Touchstone Books, 1998.

———. *D-Day June 6, 1944: The Climactic Battle of World War II.* Reprint, New York: Simon and Schuster, 1995.

Bradley, James, and Ron Powers. *Flags of Our Fathers.* New York: Bantam Doubleday Dell Publishing, 2000.

Brokow, Thomas. *The Greatest Generation.* New York: Random House, 1998.

———. *The Greatest Generation Speaks: Letters and Reflections.* New York: Random House, 1999.

Duggan, Paul. "GIs Also Fought for Social Justice." *Boston Sunday Globe,* December 17, 2000, A50–51.

Eisenhower, John S. D. *The Bitter Woods: The Dramatic Story, Told at All Echelons—from Supreme Command to Squad Leader—of the Crisis That Shook the Western Coalition.* New York: Da Capo Press, 1995.

Harwell Wells, Ann. *Always in My Heart: The World War II: Letters of Ann and Coleman Harwell.* Franklin, Tenn.: Hillsboro Press, 2000.

Hoffman, Alice M., and Howard S. Hoffman. *Archives of Memory: A Soldier Recalls World War*. Lexington: University Press of Kentucky, 1991.

Keegan, John. *The Second World War*. Reprint, New York: Penguin Books, 1990.

———. *Six Armies in Normandy: From D-Day to the Liberation of Paris*. Reprint, New York: Penguin Books, 1994.

Kryder, David. *Divided Arsenal: Race and the American State during World War II*. Cambridge: Cambridge University Press, 2000.

Merritt, Richard L., and Bruce A. Williams. *Democracy Imposed: U.S. Occupation Policy and the German Public, 1945–1949*. New Haven: Yale University Press, 1995.

Ryan, Cornelius. *The Longest Day: June 6, 1944*. New York: Touchstone Books, 1994.

Toland, John. *Battle: The Story of the Bulge*. Lincoln: University of Nebraska Press, 1999.